RETURN TO BASICS

RETURN TO BASICS

GOD'S WORD: THE FINAL AUTHORITY

BOB ELLIS

Copyright © 2021 Bob and Kathy Ellis. All Rights Reserved.

Scripture taken from the HOLY BIBLE
NEW INTERNATIONAL VERSION
Copyright 1973, 1978, 1984 International Bible Society.
Used by permission of Zondervan Bible Publishers.

"I thank Kathleen Marquardt for her diligent work in editing this book."

CONTENTS

INTRODUCTION..1

Chapter 1 Unity versus Division? 11

Chapter 2 Religion or Relationship..27

Chapter 3 Purpose of the Church?...33

Chapter 4 Purpose of Church Leadership?..................................43

Chapter 5 Savior? or Lord and Savior? 53

Chapter 6 Signs of Discipleship/Relationship? 65

Chapter 7 Doctrine? - Necessary? (if so, which?).......................77

INTRODUCTION

President Abraham Lincoln once stated, "Books teach us that our original thoughts aren't so original after all." Or as the writer of the Book of Ecclesiastes remarks several times, much of what we focus on is "meaningless" or that there is "nothing new under the sun". God describes or tells us in his word who he is. We are told, 'You are not a man that You should lie'. Your word assures us that You do not change - that You're the same today as You were yesterday and as You will be tomorrow. This book is written by a layman for laymen. It is written by a prodigal son. This book is primarily for the bride of Christ - the Church - regardless of flavor (denomination).

When prompted to answer questions about my church affiliation I describe myself as a Christian and a Bapticostal. Seeds for this book were planted on April 9, 1986. It may sound strange, especially if you don't believe that God still speaks to individuals, but God told me to write it and He gave me the title and chapter headings. He also told me He would give me the words. Because

I'm hardheaded and stubborn it's now 35 years later. This book is being written in obedience to God after a lifetime of running from His call on my life - a call I have responded to only sporadically. Is there anything special about me? Other than what God says about me, No! I was nearly aborted in 1941, but the prayers of Granny Rose touched the heart of God and He convinced my mother not to kill me. In 1943, Granny Rose prayed as she saw me fall out of a second-story window to the concrete sidewalk below. When she rushed down the stairs and reached the sidewalk, I didn't have a mark on me. I was almost two and told her a man 'catched' me. Strangely, there was no one on that Miami sidewalk. Perhaps a guardian Angel? In August of 1967, Granny Rose awoke in the wee hours of the morning and began fervently praying for me. I was in Vietnam at a fire control base about to be overrun by a vastly superior enemy force during the monsoon season. Because of the weather we could not call in air support to help us. A big, black Army 1st Sergeant began singing 'Holy, Holy, Holy' followed by 'The Battle Hymn of the Republic'. As best we could, nearly two hundred soldiers joined in singing those hymns. Miraculously the enemy forces vanished. God was there for me in 1941, 1943, and 1967. I've no doubt God has been there for me countless times since - just as He has been for you.

Let's go back to September 1959, when at the age of seventeen, I entered a pre-ministerial program at a small Christian college. I dropped out of college four months later (more on this shortly). I then ran away from home by joining the military and serving from 1960 until retiring in 1983. During those years I earned a couple of college degrees the hard way - going to school nights and weekends while working full time. I can't count the number of jobs I had after retiring - you know, 'jack of all trades, master of none'. That was a real blow to my substantial ego. For four of those years I worked at a nearby community college. My most fulfilling job was as a GED (General Educational Diploma) instructor during which time I helped several hundred adults earn a GED. Happily, several of my students went on to complete two or four-year college degrees. I was an alcoholic for about ten years. I've been divorced twice. I was estranged from my two sons for many years after divorcing their mother. During my seventy-nine years, I've served in churches as a Sunday School teacher, deacon, elder, outreach director, and pastor for a couple of small churches. I've worked in prison and jail ministries, and as a volunteer in a large suicide outreach center. I've been married to my wife Kathy for nearly thirty-four years. Kathy has the patience of Job. She describes me as a Triple-A personality. Kathy quotes Proverbs 27:17 which states that "iron sharpens iron". These words have to do with confronting each other with the truth in love. They deal with the challenge to be more than we are and have to do with accountability. At times I deal with anger, cynicism, and depression. Kathy tells me the source of my anger and depression is that I haven't given up, given in, and surrendered to God and His call on my life. In the last eighteen years, I've survived a heart attack, prostate cancer, and a few other health issues. Kathy and I are retired and enjoy a comfortable life. We live in a nice home on the lake and have no bills. Despite me being me, there are people who seem to genuinely care for me. Most of all, God hasn't given up on me. Neither has Kathy who says, "You're a work in progress." Thank you God for Your love and for Kathy's love and the blessing she is to me.

There's no shortage of books written by nationally known pastors. So, why would you bother to read this book written by a nobody? Maybe your life story is a bit like mine. I've read many great books, written by God's servants. Some of those books are scholarly - some, not so scholarly. Many of these men and women are deceased but the truth of their words lives on. That truth lives on only because it is based on God's revealed word and their relationship with Him, through the life of God's Son, Jesus. One of these books, *Adventures in Adversity*, written by Paul E. Billheimer, took over a year to read. I was at a low point in my life and at times could read only a few sentences before throwing the book to the other side of the room. Billheimer also wrote, *Destined for the Throne* - the destiny for those who know and claim Jesus as Lord and Savior. I've read several versions of the Bible. I've studied New Testament (koine) Greek and Hebrew as I've searched for answers. Whatever the reason, God continues to pursue me with relentless love, even at times when I've turned and walked away. In my journey, I've gone from fragile faith, to not believing and trying to disprove God's word (a dismal ten-year period), and finally accepting that God's word is true. When I was in the pits of despair, well-meaning friends reminded me of Romans 8:28, "all things work to the good of those who love the Lord and are called according to His purpose". At times my response was to shake my fist at God and ask for a second opinion. Today I know that God is the author and finisher of my faith. Ultimately I know it is He and not me who will complete that which He began in my life. How do I know? Because His word tells me His Son was crucified before the foundation of the Earth was laid. Jesus was crucified to cancel a debt that I could not pay. I couldn't do enough good things to earn my salvation. While works are important, works alone aren't enough. It took the shed blood of Jesus on the cross at Calvary to redeem me from the power of sin and death. God loved me and loves you that much. The book we know as The Bible is ultimately a love story and a promise book - for believers and those who reject God's word. Think eternal consequences!

Regarding God, I've concluded that people have three choices. We can run from God (disobey), or participate, mostly as spectators (think going through the motions), or dive in and commit to a moment-by-moment, 24/7 relationship. Ultimately, Christianity is all about relationship - it's not just a religion. At times in my life, I've made all three choices. In 1959, when my youthful, untried faith was confronted by a highly respected college professor with the initials ThD. after her name. She, in a single semester, explained away every miracle of the Old Testament as some evolutionary, scientific, humanistic, or natural occurrence. My thoughts? If I can't believe the Old Testament why should I believe the New Testament. I chose to run. Little did I know I was running from God. That realization only came later in life. To run from God can take the form of success by this world's standards. That can it be in the realm of education or a successful career. However, running from God oftentimes leads to a life of emptiness, divorce, drugs, alcohol, or suicide. In Psalms 139 the psalmist concludes that running from God is the ultimate exercise in futility. He asks, "Where can I flee from your presence? If I go up to the heavens, you are there; if I make my bed in the depths, you are there." In other words, you can run but you can't hide. In Jeremiah 1:5 God spoke these words to Jeremiah, "Before I formed you in your mother's womb, I knew you, before you were born I choose you". I believe those words spoken by God to Jeremiah were also directed to you and to me.

From Genesis to Revelation, it is clear that God is omnipresent. That's a theological word meaning everywhere at the same time. How can God be everywhere at the same moment in time? God being God is not limited by our concepts of time and space. He is in fact, the creator of time and space. Because He is infinite He is not subject to the limits of time and space as we (created beings) are. Truth be known, at this point in my life, I have more questions than answers. I do know that God has a purpose for every life, including yours. Isaiah 43:21 states that God's people are to "proclaim my praise." And 2 Corinthians 5:18 tells us that God, "gave us the ministry of reconciliation." If you're a Christian you share that ministry with your pastor. Contrary to what the world teaches, it's really not about you or me! It is about God and His priorities - the things that matter to God. Ultimately the only thing that matters is that which is eternal.

We are a nation of spectators. There are different levels of spectating, from casual to fanatic. Sadly many of us are also spectators in the arena of Christianity. We even have 24/7 Christian programming. While we may participate at some level of involvement (got my ticket punched), any level of participation that doesn't result in a transformed life relegates Christianity to a spectator sport. It's easy to say, I teach Sunday School or I sing in the choir or I'm a deacon or I tithe or anything else. Anything less than total commitment is dangerous in that we may settle for good when the God of creation wants the best for us. I've attended leadership conferences where I've seen church leaders respond to altar calls for salvation. To be a church leader (a church leader, the shepherd of His flock) without first accepting Jesus as Savior, can have dire consequences for the people (the flock) of God. How can you lead people into a deep relationship with God without having that relationship yourself? Can I teach you to swim if I can't swim? I may have read books on brain surgery - do you want me doing surgery to remove your brain tumor? I drove by a marquee in front of a church many years ago. The words on that marquee said, **"Christianity isn't a religion, it's a relationship."** Looking back at the First Century Church, it's obvious that Christianity wasn't a spectator sport. That is unless you watched as Christians were crucified or fed to the lions or burned at the stake. Many Christians paid the ultimate price to follow Jesus.

So, what about the choice to commit to a 24/7 relationship? The book of Matthew ends with a challenge known as the Great Commission. The disciples are told, 'Go into the World and teach them to obey all I've commanded you (to do).' Who was the 'I' who said this? None other than Jesus the Son of God who was beaten, crucified, died, and was buried - who then arose from the grave on the third day. Through his sinless life and resurrection, Jesus conquered sin and the grave. He is now seated at the right hand of God, a place of highest honor.

Several years later that Church marquee had another significant thought. It said, **"You only believe that part of scripture that you do. All else is just idle talk."** Sunday mornings Christians across this nation proclaim they believe scripture to be inspired by God, to be inerrant, to be the perfect word of God. Why don't we understand that if this is true, something is required of us? What is required? God's word challenges us to respond - to become Christ-like - to be transformed into his image. In our 21st Century mindset, we don't understand the definition of a disciple. Jesus' disciples were obedient to His teachings and carried His words throughout the world. And for their obedience, nearly every one of them died a martyr's death.

Today, rather than allowing Scripture to transform us into the image of Christ, we manipulate scripture to suit our own purposes. Rather than accepting that God's word means what it says, we often spiritualize His word with the words, "But that was then, this is now". We love to take the text out of context. By doing this we unconsciously place God in a box in a feeble effort to manipulate Him. We conform Him to our own image. However, scripture reveals to us who God is - what He is like - and what His plans are for us. One of the Ten Commandments tells us **not to worship false images**. The degree to which the God we worship does not conform to who God truly is, creates a false god - a little god.

Words are used to describe or define everything we think, see or do. The word congruent when applied to humans, simply means that people are the same regardless of the situation - they're not one thing today and another tomorrow. In reality, most of us live fractured lives. We're one thing on Sunday and someone else the rest of the week. Jesus often used the words obey and submit when speaking to his disciples. Various forms of the word Lord are used nearly 8,000 times in the Old and New Testaments. The word Lord had the meaning of owner, one who had the right to control, or one to whom obedience was owed. The people who heard Jesus speak the words command and obey understood that when a 'Lord or Master' spoke that a response was required. Our prisons and jails are overflowing with people who chose to break the laws of society, many of which are based on God's word. Their lives are guided by the lyrics of a song Frank Sinatra sang. "I Did It My Way". This book is part of that third choice - a decision to enter into an intimate relationship with a God who has only my (our) best interests at heart. God assures us in Jeremiah 29 it is His desire to bless and not harm us. A condition to receiving God's blessing requires a personal response. If we are to receive God's overwhelming blessings, then obedience, submission, and commitment are necessary responses. Think of the consequences had Jesus not submitted to God's will. He knew he was about to be arrested, tried in an illegal court, beaten, and crucified, he asked God if there was another way. Then he said, "Thy will be done." His sacrifice - His obedience bought our freedom today.

Is life a continual struggle for you? The happiest people I know have reached the end of themselves. They've given up and given in. They have surrendered. They rest from their own labors and no longer obsess with 'me, my, and mine'. They've replaced their own priorities with God's priorities. Essentially, they've decided to let go and let God.

With God's help and the leading of the Holy Spirit, the words in this book will bless you and the Kingdom of God will be enlarged. To God be all honor and glory for He alone is worthy of our praise.

CHAPTER 1
UNITY VERSUS DIVISION?

Christians have differing thoughts about unity and division, some of which have little biblical foundation. There's a saying that we evangelize through church splits. I've seen churches split over the type of music used during church services or the color of the new carpet. I've visited churches where folks sitting on one side of the aisle didn't speak to those on the other side of the aisle. Often we major in the minors rather than focusing on God's priorities. Doctrine often divides us. Is the Sabbath Saturday or Sunday? Remember **Thy Will Be Done?** Division is almost always a bad thing, while unity is considered to be positive. **But not always.** We've all heard the saying, 'united we stand, divided we fall'. Do a web search for the word unity. You'll be amazed at the countless numbers of websites that have the word unity in them. A friend who is a Baptist preacher tells me there are about sixty different Baptist denominations in the United States. We use words to define concepts such as unity and division. Unity is generally defined as oneness, being united with others to serve a greater good, complete accord among persons regarding attitudes, opinions, and intentions, or even harmony. Division on the other hand is separation resulting from differences of opinion, disagreement, or dissension. Our nation fought a long, bloody war over the issue of slavery. We fought a long police action because North Korea wanted to unify North and South Korea. Even the Vietnam conflict was an attempt at unification which was ultimately achieved by the North. Is unity always a good thing? Guess it depends on the circumstances.

The book of Genesis begins with the words, "In the beginning God". I believe those four words are the foundation of every word which follows through to the last Amen in The Book of Revelation. A Christian's mindset must begin with and end with those words. In Genesis we learn it is God's intention that a man and woman become one flesh (united) - a good thing. By the way that still is God's plan for the human race. No matter how popular, any other alternative lifestyle places the human race in danger of extinction.

Several chapters later in Genesis we learn that unity may be a bad thing. The account of Noah and the ark and the great flood has taken place. The setting is the Plain of Shinar, probably located about sixty miles south of Baghdad in Iraq. Here, all of humanity is joined together in a building project known as the Tower of Babel. Genesis 11:1-9 gives the account. Humanity is unified in its desire to build a city with a tower that reaches heaven. This tower was probably a ziggurat having a spiral staircase such as the structures discovered by archaeologists in that region. God came down to see what they were doing. Of course, God being God, already knew the what and the why of their efforts. God is omniscient - meaning he knows everything that happened before the Book of Genesis and after the Book of Revelation. While a visitation from God can be a good thing, such was not the case on the Plain of Shinar. God observed that if the people were united in this effort it would not be good because nothing they attempted to do would be impossible.

Think about the implications of that statement - NOTHING IMPOSSIBLE! Now, if your mindset is that humanity is in an evolutionary state in which we are evolving into a higher state of kindness, niceness, and love for one another - wow! It's utopia. Wonderful! No starving children, no child abuse, no sex trafficking, no drug abuse, no poverty, no wars, no genocide, solutions for aids, cancer, Alzheimer's disease, Covid-19, no crime, or any of the social ills that plague society. Again God said NOTHING IMPOSSIBLE! What could possibly be wrong with that? Nothing surprises God. Don't you think God knew about starving children? About war? Our perversions? About our diseases?

I believe God's actions at the Tower of Babel were intended to protect us from ourselves. If you truly believe the human race is evolving into a finer state of being, why is the evening news full of senseless acts of violence? History confirms that humanity is capable of heinous crimes against our fellow man. Consider Hitler and Nazi Germany with their concentration camps, gas chambers, ovens, and mass graves. We're told that Russia's Stalin caused the deaths of approximately sixty million Russians, many of whom were Jews. More recently in Cambodia, the Khmer Rouge and Pol Pot oversaw the extermination of nearly two million Cambodians (one-quarter of the Cambodian population). This occurred during the implementation of a Four Year Agrarian Plan - yet another failed utopian dream-turned nightmare. Conservative estimates tell us there have been more than sixty thousand acts of worldwide terrorism since 911. There are forces at work today in Africa intent on exterminating people, many of them Christians, who are powerless to defend themselves. Why don't the world's highly evolved, civilized societies intervene? The probability is that we really don't care because it's happening to them and not to us. More on this thought in Chapter 7.

Since Roe v. Wade became the law of the land in 1973 we've aborted sixty million innocent, defenseless babies. It is said, the most dangerous place for a baby is in the mother's womb. We (YOU & ME) as Christians support and pay for abortions. Oh yes, we do! To the tune of half a billion dollars annually! Taxes paid by Christians fund Planned Parenthood in its war against the unborn. I view the act of abortion as the sacrifice of babies on the altar of women's rights. Think about the potential for the abuse of power that total unity might bring. In 1881, England's Lord Acton stated, "All power corrupts and absolute power corrupts absolutely." Knowing that mankind is not inherently good or kind, God did something on the Plain of Shinar to prevent humanity from reaching its goal of unity. He confounded their language and dispersed them all over the world.

People often ask, "Why does God allow good people to suffer?" Maybe we need to look more closely at the word good. Jesus was approached by a man who referred to Jesus as good. Jesus rebuked the man with the words, "there is none good but my Father in Heaven". Think about that! Most of us think of ourselves as 'good people'. When I share the gospel I ask why should God allow you into his Heaven? Peoples' response? Because I'm a good person. And yet, the Son of God did not consider himself to be 'GOOD'. Would it be okay if God allowed only bad people to suffer? I don't know why God allows suffering. I used to wonder about that issue. I have come to the realization that by asking that question I essentially judge God by human standards. I don't believe He uses sickness and disease to punish us, not in the way we think of punishment. God's word repeatedly speaks of His love for us. We are assured in Jeremiah 29 that God knows the plans He has to bless us and not harm us. Ultimately, I accept that God's ways are higher than my ways. There was a 1950s radio/television series by the title, "Father Knows Best." When in doubt we need to accept in faith that the God of creation knows best. Unity may or may not be a good thing.

Let's move to the New Testament and some of the red-letter words in John 17. Jesus is near the end of His earthly ministry. He is speaking to His disciples just before entering the Garden of Gethsemane where he will be arrested and later tried, by Hebrew law, in an illegal trial. He is praying for His disciples because He knows he is about separated from them and be crucified. Jesus expresses three concerns as He prays. First He prays for himself. Secondly, He prays for His disciples that 'they may be one as we (Father and Son) are one'. This is one more thing I don't fully comprehend. It's above my pay grade. How can God and Jesus be one? Add the Holy Spirit and you have the Trinity. Talk about the ultimate in unity! And yet, Christians are divided by beliefs about the Trinity. Jesus, in Matthew 28, the Great Commission, told His disciples to baptize in the name of the Father, the Son, and the Holy Spirit. There are divisions (we call them denominations) within Christianity. Those who baptize only in the name of Jesus, reject the doctrine of the Trinity. Are we splitting hairs? Are we 21st Century legalists/Sadducees/Pharisees? In Genesis God says 'let US make man in OUR image'. When Jesus is being baptized by John, God speaks from Heaven and says, 'this is MY Son with whom I am well pleased'. Later, Jesus says to His disciples, 'I'm going away and I'm leaving the comforter (the Holy Spirit) - sure sounds like the Trinity to me. Why do we use the form of baptism to divide the Body of Christ? In John 17:20, 22&23 Jesus repeats that prayer except He prayed for His disciples (does that include you and me?). In verse 23 He asks (prays) that 'they (we) be brought to complete unity.'

God is not a serendipity kinda guy. He is always purpose-driven. In this case, unity among believers is intended. Jesus explains His purpose for unity is 'to let the world know that you (God the Father) sent me (Jesus the Son) and have loved them (every believer who would then follow His teachings)'. Then in John 17:26 Jesus prays, 'that I myself may be in them' - why does Jesus request this? He answers this question with the words, 'that the love you have for me may be in them'. If this kind of unity demonstrates love to the world, what do dissension and division within the church demonstrate? How important is unity to God? Let's see, Jesus (who is God in the flesh) knows He is about to be crucified. Some of His final words to His followers (you and me) stress the importance of being in one accord: in unity with each other.

We occasionally hear pastors speak of the importance of unity within the body of Christ. Have you ever personally experienced a church split? If your answer is in the affirmative, you know the gut-wrenching pain and emotional suffering inflicted on church members. Some victims of church splits never recover and never darken the doors of another church (building). Church splits destroy our witness. Be assured the world is watching this demonstration of Christian love (?) and fellowship. Witnesses often call us hypocrites. A hypocrite is a person who says one thing but does something else. Their walk, 'don't line up with their talk'. The only possible justification for a church split is embracing false doctrine. I think most would agree that church splits are bad. That is unless you're the person causing the split, in which case you have your own good reasons. Perhaps you're the head of a church - after all your family established and has controlled your church for the last 100 years. Scripture tells us that Christ gave His life for the Church - we are His Bride and He is the groom. We are important - we are the Church. He gave His life for you and me. Scripture identifies Jesus as the Head of His Church, and yet we call it our church. Really? There is a significant difference between His Church and my church. Oh yeah, you go to church, perhaps a beautiful building on Main Street - but, that's all it is - just a beautiful building. Jesus did not die for the sake of a building, no matter how beautiful. Hmmmm! If you're a divisive person perhaps you should live in fear and trembling.

Speaking of division, the divorce rate in the church is almost as high as it is in society at large. Counselors identify poor communication and money issues to be the most common factors in divorce. Divorce was not and is not God's plan. Think about it. Most Christians agree that divorce is not a good thing. Many unbelievers also think that divorce is bad. I'm twice divorced - DIVORCE IS NOT A GOOD THING.! There was a time when 'till death do us part meant till death do us part'. Before No-Fault Divorce, which was created by utopian social engineers, divorce was not commonplace. People were inclined to work through their so-called irreconcilable differences. Many of those forward-thinking social engineers have since looked back and admitted that the stated goal of improving the living conditions for women and children, A.D. (After Divorce), didn't materialize. Generally, it is children who suffer the most in divorces. Their world is shattered and torn apart. Children often blame themselves for causing the divorce. Children, having gone through divorce often have issues with intimacy and trust. Many of the grandiose plans foisted on society by social engineers (who believe they know better than God) result in countless unintended consequences.

God does love divorced people. And yet, many Christians and churches treat divorced people as second-class citizens. Divorce is not an unpardonable sin. When we treat people in this manner we create division in the church. In effect, we say, "I'm okay and you're not" - or worse yet, we say, "I'm worthy and you're not". Paul wrote many epistles/letters (we call them books) to the New Testament churches which addressed specific cultural issues in the early churches. Jesus and Paul always spoke in context - addressing cultural issues. Paul commented on divorce in a round-about way. I've studied the traditions, culture, customs, and history of the people to whom Jesus spoke and to whom Paul wrote his letters. Two thousand years later I wonder if we truly understand Paul's words when we read the words, 'husband of one wife'? Jesus always spoke in context to people whose culture and traditions date back to the Garden of Eden. They were and are God's chosen people. Except for some of His parables, Jesus spoke in historical/cultural context otherwise those who heard him speak would have been very confused. And yet today, we think we know exactly what Jesus and Paul meant when they spoke. Oh yeah, the only unpardonable sin? Blasphemy of the Holy Spirit. I'll leave that one to theologians and bible scholars to explain.

Ephesians 2:14 speaks of a dividing wall of hostility. Paul was in prison when writing his letter to the Church in Ephesus. Those church members were mostly Gentiles by birth. As Gentiles, they had no part in the promises God made to Abraham. Gentiles were truly outsiders. Before Jesus came Paul describes their state of being as hopeless. He reminds them of this and that it is only the blood of Christ that has broken down this dividing wall of hostility. Paul speaks both positional truth (who we are in Christ) and temporal truth (practical application of that truth to our lives). Or to express that a little differently, what we should look like and what we should be doing as followers of Christ.

Throughout his letters to the early churches, Paul uses the term 'in Christ' to define who we are and then goes on to describe what we should be doing or how we should act. In Exodus 20 God gives the Ten Commandments to the Jews. The Commandments were divided into two categories: our relationship with God and our relationship with our fellow man. Between Exodus 20 and the beginning of the New Testament when Jesus arrived in the flesh, the religious leaders had increased the original Ten Commandments to 613 laws (the mitzvot). Jesus truly understood the intentions of God when He taught 'love God and your neighbor'. He said He had come to fulfill the Law. Jesus raised the bar with His teachings. He not only saw the outside actions but also knew the inner motives. God knows our innermost secrets - secrets we hide from family and most certainly from our church family. Jesus compared anger and lust to murder and adultery. God hears the word spoken in anger. God sees that lustful look. Perhaps your wife or husband also notices that lustful look. Paul further condenses the Ten Commandments to a single command in Galatians 5:13&14. We are to serve one another in love. We are to love our neighbor as we love ourselves.

In Genesis 1:26 we find that God created man. He said, "let us create man in our image." I believe the 'OUR' spoken of is the Trinity - God The Father, God The Son, and God The Holy Spirit. I suggest that since man was created by God in His image we fulfill all of the Ten Commandments when we love our neighbor as we love ourselves. We honor the God of creation when we love people who were created by God, in His image. People are important to God as confirmed by the words in John 3:16. Remember? "For

God so loved the world that He gave His only begotten Son, that whoever believes in Him will not perish but have everlasting life."

Today, our nation is deeply divided over issues of race, abortion, diversity, political persuasion, the display of certain memorials, and immigration policies, just to name a few. The public display of the Ten Commandments, prayer at high school sports events, or simply the display of Christmas decorations is offensive to many people. Some retailers do not allow their employees to wish customers Merry Christmas fearing complaints from a few disgruntled customers. Instead, they substitute the words, Happy Holidays. We have become a nation obsessed with political correctness. We hear chants that Black Lives Matter, Blue Lives Matter, It's My Body and let's not forget the Occupy Wall Street protestors - the 95 percenters. Yes, all lives matter, including the 60 million-plus innocent babies who have been aborted. Thank you Granny Rose for your prayers and that my mother did not abort me in 1941. Consider this: if we cheapen life (abortion) at its beginning (because it's inconvenient), how long until we decide to pull the plug on our, often inconvenient, aging parents? It seems to be a natural progression of priorities. Besides, it may be that we are in debt due to our lavish lifestyle and we need the money from daddy and mommy's estate.

Both Jesus and Paul taught the importance of unity. If there is one arena where unity should be the norm rather than the exception, it is in the Church. And yet, the majority of churches are divided along racial lines. It ought not to be so. The war between the northern and the southern states ended in the Spring of 1865, nearly 150 years ago. While slavery was predominately a southern aberration, many in the north also owned slaves. Northern slaves didn't benefit (were not set free) by the Emancipation Proclamation, for a couple of years after it was enacted. General Robert E.

Lee was the Commanding General for the Confederate forces. I've been told that after the war ended, a reporter asked Lee if he believed that blacks could be saved. His response was that 'The blood at the foot of the cross was shed for all people, regardless of color.' If that is true and there truly is neither male nor female, slave nor free (God's words) - black nor white (my words) and if God's purpose is that we be united in Christ - where have we gone wrong?

It's 2021 and a wall of hostility still exists between the races in this Christian nation. There's a man of color in our men's Sunday school class who recently remarked that he wished the news media would focus on the many positive success stories and contributions of blacks in our society. Some of those influential names? Benjamin Banneker (1731-1806) was instrumental in the original survey of Washington, D.C. Booker T. Washington (1856-1915) was influential in the African American community as an educator and author, as well as in the political arena. George Washington Carver (1864-1943) was an agricultural scientist who promoted crop rotation in the South and discovered hundreds of uses for peanuts. Booker T. Washington and George Washington Carver had been slaves. Herman Cain was a very successful businessman. Dr. Ben Carson was a widely acclaimed pediatric neurosurgeon. Both Cain and Carson were presidential candidates. Alan Keyes (1950) was an ambassador to the United Nations. The list of successful blacks who have made substantial contributions to American society is endless.

About twenty years ago I was traveling with two other state employees. One was a handsome black man; a professional who was well educated. The other was an attractive blond woman, also professional and well educated. As we returned from an educational conference we stopped in a nearby city for lunch. He would not go into the restaurant and asked us to bring something out to him. Why? He was afraid to go into the restaurant in the company of a white woman. The city and county had a reputation for racism and violence against blacks. We decided to forego lunch and drive home. What's wrong with this scenario? Who is the neighbor Jesus and Paul spoke of? I wonder, does that include the victims of genocide in Africa? What about natural disasters such as hurricane Katrina. To their credit, many churches sent aid and missionary teams to assist the victims. Did we do all we could have done? Would we have done more had Katrina's victims been predominantly white? What must we do to demonstrate Christian love? Did God intend that we love and be in unity with people of color? With people from other nations? The obvious answer is **YES!**

No discussion of unity and division would be complete without consideration of the word diversity. In its broadest sense diversity simply means different. However, in our politically correct society, we often hear the word diversity (or progressive) used by social engineers who want to change society into whatever they consider to be an ideal society. The word diversity was commonplace at the community college where I worked nearly twenty years ago. In fact, during an observance of Gay Week, I was accused of defacing a student's artwork which was to be entered in an art competition. While the student's poster was offensive to me, I'm the last person who would have defaced it. I may disagree with you but I do respect and support your First Amendment right to express your opinions and beliefs - peacefully. The word diversity is, as often as not, associated with beliefs and lifestyles which attack the foundations of our Judeo-Christian nation and undermine our beliefs. I freely confess, whenever I hear the word diversity I subconsciously substitute the word perversity - diversity in the extreme.

Regarding perversity, I think back to a tee shirt worn by a male student at that community college. On it was a picture of Charles Manson and two naked women who were members of his cult. The woman sitting in the desk behind this student was offended by the shirt and complained to me. I could do nothing because of the student's First Amendment freedom of expression. Charles Manson? In 1969 Manson was the leader of a cult known as the 'Manson Family' in California made up primarily of women. In 1971 Manson was found guilty of murdering seven people and conspiring to murder two other victims and sentenced to life in prison where he died in 2017. Again, this book is not intended for the secular community. It is primarily for the Church - the Bride of Christ. It is therefore a challenge for Christians to be about God's business. Remember? THY WILL BE DONE.

I believe more is required of the men and women who comprise (not compromise) the church. I think back about twenty years to a statement made by a prominent pastor about the condition of the church. Try as I might I'm unable to identify that pastor. He said, "The problem with the church is silent pulpits and sinning saints." I believe the role of the church is to take the higher/moral/ethical ground on social issues. Many of society's ills can be traced to the church and its failure to be proactive in combating the moral decline and division in our society. Jesus called his followers (you and me) to be salt and light. In what context did He use those words? Countless sermons have been preached on the subjects of salt and light. Salt is useful for flavoring, healing, cleaning, and for preserving. Jesus asked the question, what good is salt once it has lost its flavor? He then stated once salt has lost its flavor it is good for nothing (except to be trampled underfoot). Have we become so heavenly-minded that we're no earthly good? Regarding light, we in the church sing a hymn with the words, 'This little light of mine, I'm gonna let it shine'. We are not called to hide our light but to let our light shine. I suggest for us - for Christians that salt and light are our testimony (our life/our words/our actions) as seen by the world. In that sense, every Christian is a minister and our lives are a sermon. People are watching us and they have expectations of what a Christian looks like. I often ask myself, would Jesus have done what I just did? Sadly, the answer is NO!!!

Another issue divides the church and has done so for several centuries. In First Corinthians 12 Paul addresses the issue of spiritual gifts. I know the theological teaching that these gifts given by God, were temporary in nature to testify to the authenticity of the apostles and that these gifts ended with the conclusion of the Apostolic Age. We even have a term or doctrine called cessationism to explain this thinking. Since God is not the author of confusion (1 Corinthians 14:33) why do these manifestations of the Holy Spirit divide churches? Critics of spiritual gifts always end 1 Corinthians 12 with a transition to the great love chapter (13) and end there.

Again, God is not a serendipity kinda guy; there is always an intended purpose for whatever He does or says. If you truly believe scripture is inspired by God, read Chapters 12, 13, and 14 critically and prayerfully. In Chapter 14:12 Paul encouraged the church to seek and practice the gifts that edify the church. The word edify means to build up, to encourage or benefit something; in this case, His Church. Paul used the words edify, edification, or encourage six times in Chapter 14. A technique theologians use in the study of God's word is repetition. If a word is repeated frequently it is considered to be of increased significance; e.g. Isaiah refers to God as Holy, Holy, Holy thereby emphasizing God's Holiness. Paul ends Chapter 14 with this admonition,

'Don't tell someone not to speak in tongues, whatever you do, do it in an orderly way.'

Most people reading these chapters focus on the issue of tongues (glossolalia) and gifts. However, the central focus really deals with unity within the body - the Church. Paul uses the human anatomy to illustrate his teaching. He speaks of feet, hands, ears, eyes, and the head - all are necessary for the body to be complete. He says we are Christ's body. He urges there be no division. He says we should have equal concern for each other. There have been times in my life when I felt like a hangnail, yet I was still part of the body.

Why do we take something (the gifts) given by God to the church and use it to divide the body of Christ? We say we believe the Bible to be God's revealed word. Go back to the left a couple of pages to the book of Romans, also written by Paul to a different audience. In Romans 12 Paul says something we seldom hear from the pulpit. Paul says, 'all of us form one body and that **we belong to each other**'. What a truly radical thought! I belong to you and you belong to me! As the body of Christ we belong to each other. If I understand the implications of belonging to each other, there are the issues of care and concern and accountability - and relationship. I pray for you and you pray for me. You bear my burdens and I bear yours. I help you when you need help and you help me if I need help. If we understood the concept of belonging to each other would we live life differently? Think about it!

Surveys ask people how often they attend church. The number of churchgoers is declining because many consider church to be irrelevant. Irrelevant? Think about it! I make poor choices/bad decisions/ignore God's guidelines for my life and then I blame God for the mess I'm in. Really? Christianity is not a religion, it is a relationship. If I go to church only at Christmas or Easter or once or twice a month do I have a relationship? If my wife and I live in separate houses and only see each other two or three times a year, do we truly have a relationship? Worse yet, we may live in the same house, but still have no relationship, similar to ships passing in the night. I frequently hear people say, I'm going to church. The church isn't that building down the street. That building is simply a meeting place that is **'holy ground'** only because it is dedicated to God and from time to time God graces us with his presence, in spite of our differences. It's a place where we go to fellowship with other believers as we pray for one another and seek God and His direction for our lives. While we are there we are being equipped to share the Good News and do the stuff.

The real Church is the body of Christ - His Bride. His Bride has been bought and paid for by His shed blood. His Bride (you and me) is composed of every believer who claims Jesus as Savior regardless of which meeting house they attend. We, who are Christ's body (Bride) have different personalities, skills, talents, abilities, spiritual gifts, and understandings of God's word. Regrettably, it's the latter, our understanding of God's word which divides us. While we may be sincere in what we believe, we may be sincerely wrong - life really is not about me/my/and mine. We major in the minors and forget who we are and why we're here. Our ultimate purpose is to glorify God through our actions and share the Good News of God's plan of salvation with all who will listen. This book is written by a prodigal son for other prodigal sons and daughters. It is not intended to be a deep theological treatise for those who have already arrived - where ever that may be.

CHAPTER 2
RELIGION OR RELATIONSHIP

This chapter is likely to be short. Why short? Because as my wife Kathy reminds me, "You're a work in progress" or 'God isn't finished with you yet". I still struggle with intimacy. I envy those who have truly intimate relationships with family and friends. Think about relationships!

We sing a hymn with the words, *What a Friend We Have in Jesus*. Just what is a friend? How many friends do you have? Not just hundreds of 'likes' on social media. I mean real, true friends. When I hear people say they have lots of friends I question whether they have even a single friend. It is said that if you have five friends at the time of your death you're blessed. A friend is simply someone who is there for you when no one else is. I had three such friends in my military career. Had? Time ran out for each of them. Ever had a friend who moved away? Not just to the other side of town. I mean far, far away. I envy people who have friendships that have endured the trials of time and distance. I've never attended a high school or college reunion. I've never been a joiner. I mentioned earlier that I have difficulty building enduring relationships. Some time ago a pastor's wife remarked, "Bob is a difficult person, and then she asked why he was a friend to me." His response? "Someone has to be."

I was eighteen when I learned that Mom divorced my paternal father fifteen years earlier. That's when I learned the man I'd grown up calling Pop was in reality, my step-father. He had adopted me and changed my name in court. Both his father and Mom's father (both pastors) deserted their wives, leaving them to raise their families during the Great Depression and WWII. One of them ran off to pursue a career in Hollywood - the other to be with another woman. So much for, 'til death us do part'. Moving on, my military career took me to faraway places for twenty-three years. During that time I only saw Mom and Pop during the occasional holiday while on military leave. My parents were very private people. Their business was their business. Pop was a good man and a good provider. In retrospect, he was one of the finest, most moral men I've ever known. To this day I can't remember Mom and Pop ever displaying affection to one another. Pop demonstrated love by buying nice stuff for Mom. I never really knew Mom and Pop; not the way I wish I had known them. During the Spring of 1987, I frequently called Mom and Pop but was never able to speak to Pop - there was always some reason he couldn't come to the phone. I suspected something was wrong. Then in late May I visited my parents and realized Pop wasn't well. As I was leaving to return home I hugged Pop and told him I loved him. He was very uncomfortable with my show of affection. His response still rings in my ears, "Why did you hate me?" Pop died shortly thereafter probably still believing that I hated him.

In the introduction of this book, I said that God TOLD me to write this book. Does your God speak to you? Perhaps in a still, small voice? How do you respond? Tuesday morning, August 18th, at 6:18 AM, as I was reading my bible and praying, God told me, "Leave NOW or you will never see your father again." I choose not to do that. Why? I had something (important?) to do that evening. I knew Pop was about to undergo a simple surgery the next morning and that he had heart problems. Pop died while in the recovery room on Wednesday, August 19, 1987. I saw Pop on August 20, just before he was cremated. We live with our choices.

In the years after Pop's death, I became increasingly aware of Mom's 'strange' moments. Finally, I realized that Mom was suffering from paranoid schizophrenia and dementia, as had two of her older sisters. My half brothers are five and seven years younger than me and I never really knew them (except as pests) before I left home to join the military. Psychologists tell us we learn to be husbands and wives and parents from our parents who learned these skills by watching their parents. I assumed my family was fairly typical. Only after retiring from the military did I realize that was not the case. I have since learned of a family curse spoken by two of Granny Rose's (Mom's mother) sisters who were witches and were also into voodoo and the black arts. My paternal father was a womanizer. Scripture says, 'the sins of the father are visited upon the third and fourth generations'; i.e. generational curses. Being a member of a New Testament Church which largely relegated the Old Testament to the status of some quasi-mythical/historical account of God's dealings with His chosen people, the Jews, I certainly didn't believe in generational curses. After all, that was Old Testament stuff! **Hmmm!** A higher than average incidence of alcoholism, drug overdoses, suicides, fatal accidents, lots of divorces, chronic depression, and paranoid schizophrenia has convinced me otherwise. The Old Testament is as timely for us today as it was when it was unfolding. We're assured that God is the same today as He was yesterday and as He will be tomorrow. God doesn't change. Additionally, God is not a man that He should lie. That is God's testimony about himself. His word (The Bible) is a book of His promises to us. We have the freedom to accept or reject His words and the manifold promises therein. It's a matter of choice. You can choose a little god (false god) or the great big God of creation who spoke into existence all that we can perceive with our five limited physical senses.

This chapter is all about relationships; our relationship with God and with others. One of the Ten Commandments (given by God) tells us to have no other gods but Him. Some of the other gods we might worship our possessions, power, position, jobs, education, sports, health, and wealth just to name a few. These gods are little gods which can vanish in a moment of time. Often these little gods displace the God of creation as the focus of our worship. I suggest the degree to which the god we worship does not line up with whom God reveals himself to be in scripture, is the degree to which we worship a false god. If we worship a false god there is no foundation upon which to build an intimate personal relationship. When we sing *What a Friend We Have in Jesus* I often wonder do we truly think of Jesus as a friend. Or are those words just some form of feel-good, spiritual mumbo-jumbo? I think much of what we do in church is at a shallow, perhaps emotional level. We have those warm fuzzy feelings while in the presence of other believers - but then? We leave church and return to our day-to-day lives not giving another thought to God or our church family until we return the following Sunday. Essentially, we got our ticket punched on Sunday and life goes on. And yet, Paul's words in Romans 12 say that we belong to each other - I belong to you and you belong to me. This thought suggests commitment, accountability, and an intimate relationship. Do we know the hurts and pains our church family is dealing with? Their sons or daughters or other family members who are in a bad relationship? or battling addictions? or financial struggles? or physical problems? How many times have we promised to pray for a situation or concern, only to fail to do so? Do we really care?

Friendship (relationship) is a bit like a garden. You have to invest time and energy to cultivate a relationship. Think of your time and energy as seeds planted in a garden. Friends and family are important as are other relationships. In the years since Mom died, I've spent more time on the phone with my brothers. I've driven to visit them and gotten to know and respect them as brothers. Between December 2019 and February 2020 I drove nearly 4,000 miles helping my brother Larry, recover from a stroke. It's all about caring and being there for others.

And speaking of family, did I mention my two sons? When their mother and I divorced I partially blamed them for the divorce. At Christmas of 1981, I was transferred to a new military assignment. At that time I essentially disowned them and for several years we had no contact - no relationship. God has restored our relationship. While my sons and their families live in distant states we do spend time on the phone. Late in life, I've discovered two things that bring me great pleasure: gardening and relationships. Both require that you invest yourself - your time and energy to reap the benefits.

God is in the relationship/restoration business. There was a time when Adam and Eve walked (fellowshipped) with God in the cool of the garden. As told in Genesis 3, that intimate relationship was broken when they sinned (disobeyed) God. Essentially, Satan tempted Eve to disobey God, and then she influenced her husband Adam to do likewise. If we fast forward to the New Testament, God through His Son Jesus provides a source of restoration for those who make that choice. The choice? To accept Jesus as our Lord and Savior. When we do so we are adopted into God's family. When you read Chapter 6 you'll discover there is a legal basis for our adoption as sons and daughters. Ultimately, our choice deals with our eternal destination - heaven or hell. There's a little more on the issue of relationships in Chapter 3.

CHAPTER 3

PURPOSE OF THE CHURCH?

The question is "WHY?" Why do we do what we do the way we do it? We're programmed from birth to respond to authority figures without asking WHY? The answer to this unasked question is 'Because I said so." We learn early in life that failing to follow orders may have negative consequences. Who are these authority figures? They're parents, teachers, scoutmasters, little league coaches, drill sergeants, and employers. Essentially, we see the man or woman in the pulpit as an authority figure. They are paid professionals sort of like police officers, doctors, college professors, or lawyers. In essence, pastors are salespeople - **sort of.** They're selling eternal life and fire insurance policies - as in, choose life or death - heaven or hell. For many people today the Church is increasingly considered to be irrelevant. It fails to address (solve) their personal problems - many of which are the result of their poor choices. Pastors also are leaving the ministry at an alarming rate. In this age of megachurches and televangelism, church membership is also declining at an alarming rate. Perhaps the time has come for us to ask and answer some probing questions. Why do Christians do what we do? Why do Christians do what we do, the way we do it? Are we doing something wrong? To coin a phrase, "What's it all about Alfie?" What's it all about? How did we get to be the way are - speaking of the Church.

Guess we first need to define the word Church. The Greek word used in the New Testament is *ekklesia* and appears more than one hundred times. *Ekklesia* is defined as 'a called-out assembly'. An *ekklesia* was a local body of believers who were followers or disciples of Jesus. Did I say local body of believers? It grieves me when I see the bumper sticker, 'A Church Alive Is Worth The Drive'. If you drive 50 or 60 miles to attend a church is there any accountability? Do you know the needs of the elderly? Or the widows? Or the homeless? Do you fellowship with other church members? Do you have a relationship therein? How many ministry opportunities are missed when you live so many miles away? What is your motive for driving that far?

Sadly for the majority of Christians today, church is the building where we go on Sunday; i.e. we're going to church. Or perhaps, Saturday. Think about the question people ask, "Where do you go to church?" Needless to say, we're proud of our building. It's the place we sacrificed (building fund) to erect. It may have a marquee out front with catchy sayings (sometimes offensive - even to Christians), a street address, a website, a mailbox number, and a zip code. My first response is that church, as opposed to the REAL CHURCH, is merely a meeting place or building where we go to hear a paid performer, who we call pastor or preacher or minister or father or bishop or even reverend. That building often sits empty, except for the office staff and perhaps daycare center, about ninety percent of the time. Let that thought sink in? We spend a ton of money to build and maintain an empty building.

We even sing about, "Standing on Holy Ground". In the sense that building is dedicated to God and the worship of God and the education of God's people, that building is considered to be a Holy place. If the presence of God is in that place then it truly is Holy Ground. And yet that empty building is not the Church. God did not send His Son, Jesus Christ to give His life for an empty building - no matter how dazzling - no matter how much we paid for it - no matter how proud of it we are.

The 'CHURCH' is who you and I are in and through the shed blood of Jesus. The Apostle Paul, in his letters to the early Church referred to the Church (the body of believers) with Jesus Christ (the head) as a mystery. This mystery was not revealed to the Jews in the Old Testament. Paul identifies Christ as the Bridegroom - as the head of the Church. We're identified as the Bride of Christ. We'll eventually attend a marriage celebration. Why do we exist? Is it mere ritual and tradition or do we exist for a purpose? Do we have a divinely appointed mission in life?

Before addressing that issue, there is an additional Greek word that is of significance in defining the Church and its activities. The word is *koinonia* and its derivatives are used about 20 times in the New Testament. The word is used to indicate a state of fellowship and caring - of an intimate concern for fellow believers. It's about relationships. The first deacons were table waiters who cared for the needs of widows and orphans, thereby freeing the elders or overseers of the Church to attend to the spiritual affairs of the Church. As I've expressed this thought to other Christians their response often is, "But that was then, this is now." The Apostle Paul, the guy who God used to pen much of the New Testament, wrote a letter to the Christians in Rome. In Romans 12:5 he stated that 'Christians belong to each other'. If I understand these words correctly, I belong to you and you belong to me. What a radical thought. Gee! that smacks of accountability. Ah, but that's just more of 'that was then, this is now stuff'. We seem to miss the importance of that thought. Hmmmm! Maybe that's why we find it so easy to evangelize the World through division or church splits. As Jesus did, Paul also repeatedly calls for unity within the Body of Christ. If we go back to the Upper Room we are told that the disciples 'were together in one accord'. I don't think that was a Japanese automobile! Paul repeatedly states that we are to think more highly of others (not just other Christians) than we do of ourselves. Gee whiz! And all this time I thought it was all about me/my/and mine. Christianity really has some truly radical thoughts if we dare take it seriously. Therein lies the problem.

Perhaps we need to stop and ask an existential question - why do we exist? Are we here - 'just poof and we're gone'? Or is there a greater purpose to be served? God speaking through the prophet Isaiah proclaimed that He had, "formed a people for Himself that they may proclaim His praise." In other words, we exist to praise and glorify God while here on Earth, and eventually, we will become the Bride of Christ. If you're a man, you probably have trouble comprehending being a bride - I do. I've been the groom three times - never a bride. Remember the red words? They were spoken by the guy who dared to proclaim to the World that He is the Son of God. In Matthew 26:64 Jesus tells His accusers, "Yes, I am the Son of God". In other words, the Son existed with the Father and with the Holy Spirit. They pre-existed before time began - before the beginning of the Book of Genesis. Remember the words, "Let us make man in our own image." God the Father, God the Son, and God the Holy Spirit are antecedent - meaning they existed before all else. They were and are eternal - no beginning and no end. Do I understand all of this? NO! That's where faith comes in. Do I fully understand God? NO!

John testifies to this in John 1:1-18. There, Jesus was referred to as the WORD, who pre-existed with God (before the act of creation) and who then created ALL that we, with our physical limitations, can perceive with our five senses. Those senses deal with the material world. Is there a sixth sense? A spiritual sense?

God tells us that He is 'Spirit' and that those who would worship Him must do so in spirit and truth. Do we worship God 'in spirit and in truth' when we show up a couple of times each month? Is more required and expected? Surveys indicate that only about 18 percent of church members tithe. The OT book of Malachi says we rob God when we fail to tithe. Surveys also indicate that only about 18 percent of church members are active in some support role - teaching, singing in the choir, vacation bible school, bus ministry, feeding the hungry, community outreach programs, or workdays at church. What does it mean to worship God 'in spirit and in truth'? Does it not mean, "walkin' the walk and not just talkin' the talk"? Does it not mean being used by God to reach out and help those who need our help? How about the little old lady down the street who needs her grass cut? Or was her wheelchair ramp rebuilt? Or a ride to Church? Or someone to help with her shopping? Or a ride to the doctor or dentist's office. Or participating in a jail or prison ministry? Or volunteering at a homeless shelter?

Theologians describe God as being Omniscient. That simply means that God knows everything there is to know and He knows it before it happens. Wow! Picture God as the fountain of wisdom and knowledge. Proverbs 1:7 states, "The fear of the Lord is the beginning of knowledge, but fools despise wisdom and discipline." The word fear in this scripture has the meaning of honor, respect, revere, or highly esteem. My understanding of the word knowledge deals with facts while wisdom deals with how you use or apply facts. Even before God created Adam He knew that Adam would sin in the Garden of Eden. Adam's sin came as no surprise to God. God didn't start wringing His hands and begin crying 'woe is me - what have I done?' He didn't go into some frenzied, 'what now?' panic attack. God already had the plan of salvation and, NO, that plan was not the Ten Commandments, or the Jewish sacrificial system, or the Jewish mitzvot with its 613 laws. God's PLAN A - God's only plan has many names - the Rose of Sharon, the Lily of the Valley, the Lion of Judah, Emmanuel (God with us), Messiah, Jesus Christ, the King of Kings, the Lord of Lords, and the Alpha and the Omega, just to name a few. God knew before the World was created that Judas Iscariot would betray Jesus (His Son) for 30 pieces of silver. God's word even states that Jesus was chosen/crucified before the foundation of the World was laid (1 Peter 1:20 and Revelation 13:8). Many doubting Thomases believe that Jesus was Plan B implemented after Plan A, the Ten Commandments and the mitzvot (613 additional laws) failed. The coming of Jesus is foretold in the Old Testament in many places, but specifically by the prophet Isaiah in Isaiah 61:1-3. Jesus uses the same words as reported by Luke 4:14-21 to describe Himself. Jesus was addressing the Jews in the Synagogue in Nazareth on the Sabbath and stated that He was the fulfillment of Isaiah's prophecy.

Dr. Peter Stoner, in his book, *Science Speaks* uses the science of probability to examine prophecies in the Old Testament which were fulfilled in the birth, life, death, and resurrection of Jesus Christ. People who play poker, who bet on the greyhounds and thoroughbred horses, who bet on the outcome of major sporting events use probability to determine their chances of winning big bucks. The probabilities against so many prophecies being fulfilled in the life of a single person (Jesus) are astronomical. A gambler would not place a $2 bet against such high odds - he certainly would lose and yet Jesus fulfilled every prophecy spoken of Him in the Old Testament.

God always has a purpose - there is no coincidence or serendipity in God. God's purpose is clearly stated in both the Old and New Testaments. If then, Jesus came to do something, and if then, we are His disciples, and if then, He is today seated at the right hand of God His Father (also known as Abba), and if then, He left us to do something - what should we be doing? What should we look like? Is it enough to go to church once, twice, or three times a month and get our ticket punched? It's really not about the sponge mentality. It's not about 'sittin and soakin'. It's about 'doin' something'. Remember? Thy will be done.

It's about being obedient to the Great Commission given by Jesus in Matthew 28:18-20. Herein Jesus (The Master) states, "All authority in heaven and earth has been given to me." Think about the implications of 'all authority in heaven and earth is mine'. With this statement, Jesus establishes his 'bona fides' - the legal/lawful/legitimate basis for what he is about to say to his disciples. Authority given by whom? Obviously by God his father. Jesus then orders (not asks), his disciples, "Therefore (now) go make disciples and teach them to obey all that I have commanded you". I suspect the words (obey and command) used by Jesus are really, really important words. While they are significant words, I suspect most of us within the Church minimize the importance of these words. After all, we're the New Testament Church and we're covered by the blood of Jesus and by God's grace and mercy because we publicly confessed with our mouths, Jesus to be our savior. Really?

People called Jesus, Lord. A Lord might have the power of life and death over his subjects. Jesus, the master and teacher, had twelve disciples. In the Jewish culture, a true disciple was expected to be a duplicate of his teacher. A disciple walked like, talked like, and did the same things his teacher did. If you're not sure about this Great Commission it is further described by Luke in Luke 24:47 (more Red Letters) - repentance and forgiveness will be preached. The Apostle Paul also addresses the Great Commission in 2 Corinthians 5 wherein Paul tells us 'we all have the ministry of reconciliation'. You may say, "Oh, but I'm not a minister. Besides, that's what we pay our preacher to do". If you're a true Christian then you're a Christ-follower and a disciple. If you're a disciple you're supposed to be doing more than acquiring knowledge in the form of chapters and verses of scripture. It's more than a knowledge of Greek and Hebrew. It's more than knowing the history and the geography of Israel. It's more than knowing the culture and traditions of the Jewish people. It's about living and applying God's word to your life. As a disciple of Christ and member of God's family, it's about sharing the Good News, the Gospel of Jesus Christ with your family, your friends, your neighbors, your co-workers, the clerk at the store, and perfect strangers. It's about the practical application of God's Word to our lives. Anything less is to accept a lie - to live a lie - ultimately to die in deception and then perhaps to spend eternity (a long, long, really long time) in hell. Jesus had a lot to say about hell. Don't believe in hell? Sorry, it's not your plan and you're really not the boss.

So, what's it all about? It doesn't take a rocket scientist to know what we should be doing - just read Isaiah 61:1-3 and the words of Jesus in Luke 4:14-21 and Matthew 28:18-29. Read the Beatitudes and the Golden Rule about 'doing unto others'. But, you say, 'I've never killed anyone or committed adultery'. Have you ever looked at a woman or a man with impure thoughts in your mind? Our 38th President, Jimmy Carter acknowledged the truth of these words. How about anger? Are you angry with someone? Jesus had a way of cutting through all of our self-righteousness. He said you're guilty of adultery by lusting after a woman to whom you're not married. He said you're guilty of murder by being angry with someone. Jesus raised the bar, thereby setting a higher standard for those who follow Him. Jesus said love God and your neighbor. Scripture tells about a rich young guy who came to Jesus with the question, "What must I do to inherit the Kingdom of Heaven?" Jesus said, "Keep the laws." The rich guy responded, "This I've done since I was a youth." Jesus knew his heart and said, "Then sell all you have and give it to the poor and follow me." The rich guy walked away sadly and is never heard of again. It's really simple stuff! Do I understand it all? Nope!

I no longer ask the question, "Where did God come from?" It is only when I acknowledge that God truly is who His word says He is, that I begin to have some limited understanding of who God is and how I am to respond to Him. I do know that the God who said to Moses, "I AM THAT I AM" is not accountable to me or to you. He is supreme. He is sovereign. He WAS, IS, and FOREVERMORE will be God with no beginning and no end. Speaking of The Word, I have come to the conclusion the most significant words in the Bible are found in Genesis. All the words in the Old and New Testament and in Christianity hang on four foundational words. Christianity is based on our understanding and acceptance of these words. The words are, "In the beginning GOD". More on this later.

CHAPTER 4

PURPOSE OF CHURCH LEADERSHIP?

As I've said before, God is not a serendipity kinda guy. In recent years we've heard of 'purpose driven' this and that. With God, purpose is not something new. Purpose has always been God's intention. God's plan has not changed from before He began creation as we know it. Everything from, "In the beginning God" to the "Amen", the last word in the Book of Revelation, was known to God and was his ultimate plan.

We all have ideas about who God is and what He is like. Three of the many words theologians use to describe the God of Creation are: Omniscient, Omnipresent, and Omnipotent. These words are difficult for the human mind to comprehend and must be accepted in faith. **Omniscient** means that God knows everything before it happens. He knew before creating Adam that he would sin, thereby breaking fellowship with God. I also believe God knew your name before he created time and space and the world as we know it. **Omnipresent** means God is everywhere at the same moment of time. Simultaneously, he hears my prayers and your prayers although we may be worlds apart. Your prayers are no less important to God than mine. **Omnipotent** means that God is all-powerful. He is in fact, the source of all power. God spoke and it happened. God merely spoke into existence everything we are able to perceive with our five senses. He also knew the Ten Commandments and the Jewish sacrificial system could not and would not save humanity from its inherited sin nature which began in the Garden of Eden. The Old Testament is full of types and shadows (not the real thing), of something to be fulfilled in the New Testament - in the personhood of Jesus.

Here's a simple example of this concept. The thirty-year-old black walnut trees in our yard cast shadows, but the shadows are not the real thing. The first blood sacrifice recorded in God's word was after God confronted Adam and Eve in the garden when they tried to hide their nakedness from Him after eating the forbidden fruit. God confronted them with the words, 'Who told you, you were naked?' God then killed an animal and used its skin to provide a covering (clothing) for their nakedness - essentially a blood sacrifice. In reality, this act was a type or shadow to be fulfilled by Jesus and his shed blood. The Jewish law and sacrificial system were also types and shadows. Many books have been written on Old Testament types and shadows to be fulfilled by Jesus in the New Testament. In the late Third Century, Saint Augustine of Hippo stated, "The new (testament) is in the old contained; the old (testament) is in the new explained." Another way of saying this is, 'Scripture interprets Scripture'.

Two additional attributes of God are that He does not lie, nor does He change. This is His testimony about himself and is stated in Numbers 23 and Malachi 3. Let's also consider testimony about

God Incarnate (God in the flesh), Jesus Christ. In John 10 Jesus says 'I and my Father are one'. Then in Hebrews 13 Paul states, Jesus is the same today as He was yesterday and as He will be in the future. It does appear that God the Father and God the Son have a lot in common.

Thousands of years pass after Adam and Eve sin in the Garden of Eden before we are introduced to a baby born to a carpenter's family in Bethlehem. This is the baby Old Testament prophets spoke of repeatedly. These prophets foretold the circumstances of this baby's birth, life, and death in great detail. This son was born to Joseph, a carpenter, and Mary, a virgin. How can it be that a virgin gives birth? This son is known as Emmanuel (God with us). This story unfolds in the New Testament books of Mathew, Mark, Luke, and John. Each of these accounts, written by different authors, is told from different perspectives and is addressed to different audiences. The story continues throughout the remainder of the New Testament, much of which is attributed to the Apostle Paul. Paul was known as Saul before he and Jesus had an eyeball-to-eyeball confrontation on the Damascus Road. Saul was well educated and respected among the Jews, having been educated by Gamaliel, a highly respected teacher of the law. Paul described himself as a Pharisee of Pharisees. In other words, he was equal to any of the Jewish leaders who demanded that Jesus be crucified. The followers of Jesus continued to increase in numbers after his crucifixion on the cross and his resurrection. Saul was authorized by the Jewish leaders to persecute (kill) the followers of Jesus. These people were not yet known as Christians. They were identified in the book of Acts as people of the 'Way'. Jesus caused Saul to be blinded as he traveled on the Damascus Road. A couple of days later Paul's vision was restored and he was forever a changed man. What and how did this encounter change Saul from one who persecuted Jesus' followers, to become a leader within the Church? Paul's letter to the Church in Corinth (2 Corinthians 12) speaks of a man, whether in spirit or in the flesh who was taken to the third heaven where wondrous things were revealed to him - things he could not reveal. Have you ever wondered how Paul, who was zealous in his persecution of Jesus' followers, then became a primary leader in the First Century Church? Where did Paul get his deep insight into what Christians should look like - what we should be doing? I believe Paul was the man he spoke of who was taken up to the third heaven. How else could Paul have understood God's plan to organize and establish the Church? By the way, after his conversion experience on the Damascus Road, Paul became the most hated man among the Jewish leaders.

Leaders in the early Church were initially known as elders. These leaders were responsible for the spiritual oversight of the Church. The Book of Acts also referred to as the Acts of the Apostles, tells about the rapid growth of the Church. There came a time when caring for the needs of widows became burdensome, thereby drawing elders away from their primary responsibility: being the spiritual leaders of the Church. I was a family deacon and outreach director for a large college and career group. As I studied the book of Acts, I discovered therein the first deacons were servants - table waiters for widows. Herein my special status was reduced to that of a servant - a table waiter.

In his letter to the Church in Ephesus 4:11-16, Paul identified several offices or positions within the Church. In this letter, God speaking through Paul spells out his purpose and intentions for the Church. Before we look at Paul's letter to the Ephesians, let's go back to Matthew 28:18-20 wherein we find the Great Commission given by Jesus to his followers. Jesus has done that which he came to do. He has been obedient to fulfill his Father's will. He shed his blood to make us (you and me) acceptable to God. Jesus is about to leave his disciples and ascend to Heaven where he is to be seated in a place of ultimate honor - at the right hand of his Father God. To his followers, Jesus said all authority in heaven and earth was his, given to him by God. The last words he spoke to his disciples were 'go into all the world, make disciples, and teach men and baptize them in the name of the Father, the Son and the Holy Spirit'. Was he speaking only to his twelve disciples (minus Judas)? Or only to pastors, elders, deacons, and others in Church leadership roles in 2021?. Or was the Great Commission given to all (you and me) who would subsequently be known as Christians? What is our role and purpose in God's eternal plan of Salvation. The time we spend in Christian conferences, reading Christian books, in revivals, in Sunday School, and listening to sermons from the pulpit or watching Christian television ultimately has purpose. It's similar to military basic training. That purpose is to equip us and challenge us to reach out to friends and family and neighbors and share the good news about Jesus and his Father in heaven. At times I wonder if we understand we have a responsibility that goes beyond just showing up at Church? Paul said 'we all have the ministry of reconciliation. Reconciliation? The act of being reconciled (restoring a right relationship) between fallen, sinful individuals and the Holy and Righteous God of creation. We have a responsibility to share the Gospel with those we meet in life.

Paul states in Ephesians 4:11-16, "and he (Christ) gave some to be apostles, some to be prophets, some to be evangelists, some to be pastors and some to be teachers, to equip his people for works of service, so that the body of Christ may be built up until we all reach unity in the faith and knowledge of the Son of God and become mature, attaining (transformed) to the whole measure of the fullness of Christ. Then we will no longer be infants, tossed back and forth by the waves, and blown here and there by every wind of teaching and by the cunning and craftiness of people in their deceitful scheming. Instead, speaking the truth in love, we will grow to become in every respect the mature body of Hhim who is the head, Christ. From Him the whole body, joined and held together by every supporting ligament, grows and builds itself up in love, as each part does its work." This scripture smacks of a team effort - not a Lone Ranger sorta thing!

The highlights of these six verses spell out the purpose Christ had for His Church - it's not my church, nor is it your church. We who claim to be Christians - followers of Jesus are His Church. Being the Head of the Church, He established these five leadership positions within His Church and goes on to identify exactly why these positions were created - again purpose and intention are spelled out!

- to equip us for works of service
- to build up the body of Christ
- to reach unity in Christ
- to become mature becoming Christlike
- that we no longer be infants
- that we not accept false teaching
- that we speak the truth in love
- that the whole body be joined together
- that we be built up in love
- as each part does its work

Note that works of service and unity and maturity and love within the body (His Church) are the focus of these verses.

Nowhere do we find 'sittin and soakin' in the words Paul wrote to the Church in Ephesus. And to us today! More on the importance of works in Chapter 7.

Paul wrote two letters to Timothy. In his first Letter Paul lists the characteristics/qualifications of Church leaders. In his second Letter he warned of a coming time when people would ignore sound doctrine. Paul listed many characteristics of these people: self-centered, mean-spirited, rebellious, pleasure seekers, appearing to be godly but indifferent to God and hence powerless. Powerless? To do what? To be His Church and to do that which we are supposed to be doing. Paul counseled Timothy to have nothing to do with these people. The Old Testament Prophet Isaiah, nearly 800 years before the birth of Jesus warned of a coming day when 'good will be called evil and evil will be called good'. Again, 'Scripture interprets Scripture'.

Paul also warned of a time when people will select church leaders who will say what they want to hear (tickle their ears), not necessarily to be taught the truth revealed in God's word. What do you know about Timothy? History tells us that Timothy was the Bishop of the Church in Ephesus. As such he was not a casual spectator. At the age of 80 Timothy was dragged through the streets and stoned to death in 97 A.D. Why? Because he protested a pagan celebration honoring the Greek Goddess Artemis also known as Diana among the Romans.

A small group met for a meal and bible study in our home for about eighteen months. One of the members said he had no need of a teacher because the Holy Spirit was his teacher. That said, I wondered why he bothered coming to our home. Perhaps he enjoyed the food and may have been lonely. I confronted Bill with this question, "If Jesus thought teachers were needed for His Church, why then did he think he had no need of a teacher?"

He was unable to answer that question. Months later he left the group. Several years later we bumped into each other and he told me he enjoyed the time in our small group and had grown a lot since then. Most importantly, he said he was more tolerant and less judgmental of other Christians. Christians have the honor and privilege of sharing in the ministry which Jesus left us. It may be that our life - our witness will be the only sermon many people will hear.

I close this chapter with some questions. Paul in Ephesians 4 identifies five leadership positions within the church; positions created and given by Jesus. Christians accept that there are pastors, evangelists, and teachers within the Church. What of apostles and prophets? There are denominations today which have within their hierarchy, the position of apostles. Recently, a pastor asked if I knew any apostles or prophets. Depending on the flavor (think denomination) of your Christianity do you accept there may still be apostles and prophets among us? In the early Church, it was expected that signs, wonders, and miracles be manifest in the ministries of apostles. Many Christians today are taught that the position of apostles and prophets ceased to exist at the end of the First Century, known as the Apostolic Age. I suspect the absence of signs, wonders, and miracles in the lives of today's apostles is reason to doubt the authenticity of his or her apostleship. Signs, wonders, miracles? That's a whole 'nother' book.

Oh yeah, the penalty for being a false prophet was death by stoning. How do you judge whether prophecy is true or false? If it doesn't happen, it's false. But, is there a time limit or expiration date on the fulfillment of any spoken prophecy? At what point do we pick up the big rocks? Old Testament prophets spoke hundreds of prophecies foretelling the coming of Jesus long before his birth in Bethlehem. I'm sure critics scoffed at the words of these prophets, perhaps even considered stoning them. Remember the Jewish religious leaders demanded the death of Jesus. If Jesus visited your church this Sunday would you recognize Him/welcome Him? Enough said on prophets and prophecy!

CHAPTER 5
SAVIOR? OR LORD AND SAVIOR?

Warning: Some may be quick to label me a heretic for the thoughts I express in this chapter. With that warning, I hope you'll read on and then decide for yourself if there is truth in these words. I think back to a 16th Century monk and priest, Martin Luther who is credited with discovering the grace spoken of in Paul's letter to the Church in Rome. Luther was excommunicated by the Pope when he challenged the Roman Catholic church for some of its practices; including the selling of indulgences for the deceased. For his teachings, Luther was labeled a heretic. This roque priest is credited with beginning the Protestant Reformation. Later in life Luther suggested that the absence of a changed life, subsequent to a salvation experience, was cause to question a man's salvation. Martin Luther died, an exile from the church.

The letters written by Paul to the First Century churches comprise much of the New Testament. When he wrote his second letter to Timothy, Paul said that all scripture is inspired by or breathed by God. The New Testament didn't exist when Paul wrote these words, therefore it is obvious Paul was referring to the Old Testament. I've often wondered, did Paul consider his letters to the early Churches, equal in authority to God's words in the Old Testament, to be, in fact, scripture? While Paul, a highly educated Jew, described himself as a 'Pharisee of Pharisees', was he so vain as to consider his words to the early church to be scripture? Moreover, would Jewish converts who were familiar with the Old Testament, who then read his letters have considered his writings to be the equivalent of scripture?

What about the 'Red Letter words' in our bibles? Have you ever wondered where we got the Red Letter bible? Was it always so? Prior to 1899, there was no Red Letter bible as we know it. It was Louis Klopsch, editor of *The Christian Herald* magazine, who we have to thank for the first Red Letter New Testament published in 1899. Many Christians have never questioned its origin, perhaps believing there has always been a 'Red Letter' bible. Christians generally consider the 'Red Letter words' to be the actual words spoken by Jesus during his earthly ministry. Perhaps we assumed that 'Red Letter' bibles always existed. Are the "Red Letter words' more important than the black words? Remember, there are no red words in the Old Testament. Do you consider yourself to be a New Testament Only Christian?

There is a concept taught in schools of theology and other places of higher learning which states that 'scripture interprets scripture'. Scripture is clear on the issue of sin and salvation. There was a time when Adam and Eve walked (fellowshipped) with God in the cool of the garden. Can you imagine walking with God sans clothing - no awareness of your nudity? Adam and Eve were influenced by Satan to sin (doubt) God, thus breaking their relationship with the God of creation. Does it seem fair that several thousand years later we should be condemned for their disobedience and rebellion? Fair? Fairness? If I even ask about fairness, I'm guilty of judging God by human standards. Who are we to judge God who first revealed himself with the words, "In the beginning God"? God's word tells us that sin entered the World through one man, Adam (not Eve), although God's stated intent was that Adam and Eve become 'one flesh'. And that one man, God's Son, defeated sin and death. Jesus was severely beaten in an attempt to appease religious leaders and the mob. In spite of the declaration of his innocence and the savage beating he received, people demanded he be crucified. The Roman governor, Pontius Pilate would have freed Jesus but the mob demanded that a violent murderer, Barabbas, be set free and that Jesus be executed in his place. After Jesus' death, his lifeless body was removed from the cross and placed in a borrowed tomb. Religious authorities feared his body might be stolen by his followers because Jesus said he would be raised up in three days. Hence his tomb was guarded by soldiers to prevent this from happening. Three days later death and sin were conquered when Jesus emerged from the tomb alive. Christians refer to that event as the resurrection which we celebrate at Easter.

Why did Jesus, who had done nothing but good, submit to all of this? He chose to be obedient to God. He was God's Plan A - to pay a debt for my sins - for your sins - something we are unable do. Doesn't matter that we think we've been good people. In Matthew 19, Jesus rebuked a man who called him good master. Jesus responded, "There is none good but my father in Heaven." We need to remember these words of Jesus when we think we are good and that our goodness will get us into heaven. God's prophet Isaiah in Isaiah 5 warned of a coming time when people would call 'good, evil and evil, good'. We can't earn our salvation by good works. We can't buy or pay for life everlasting. We can't provide enough food and shelter to enough homeless people to earn life eternal. We can't go on enough mission trips to foreign countries to buy eternity with God in heaven. Granted these are good works - works (perhaps salt and light?) expected of Christ's followers. But, works are not the basis of our salvation. Paul, in Ephesians 2:8&9, explained that we are saved by grace, an unmerited (undeserved/unearned) gift given by God and not earned by our works, lest we boast (brag) about what we've done. It took the shed blood of God's Son, Jesus Christ to wash our sins away and buy our eternal security. Therein was God's mercy, grace and love made manifest.

But! What about works? Are works important? Think of works as evidence - as fruit brought about by our new life in Christ. In Matthew 20:1-16 we find Jesus' parable of the workers in the vineyard. Workers are called by the master (Jesus?) in the early morning, who then calls others at 9, more workers are called at 12 noon, still more workers are called at 3 in mid-afternoon, and finally a group of workers are called late in the day at about 5. The master asks this group, "Why have you been standing around here all day long and done nothing?" Their response? "Because no one has hired us." The master then instructed (hired) them, "You also go work in my vineyard." Of significance, those in the 5 o'clock group received the same wages (a denarius - about 14 cents) as those who worked from the early morning hour. An aside: is a verbal response (confession of faith) to an altar call all that is required? Or is a pastor responsible for explaining to new Christians that more is expected of them? More? Is part of a pastor's responsibility, metaphorically speaking, to hire and equip workers to work the field? This parable ends with the words, "The last will be first, and the first will be last." Do I comprehend everything in God's word? NO!

Paul in Ephesians 2:20, states, "For we are God's workmanship, created in Christ Jesus to do good works, which God prepared in advance for us to do." Does God expect that Christians - do good works? Hummm? We're God's workmanship. Created in Christ Jesus to do good works. Good works, which God prepared in advance for us to do? Paul reminds us in Hebrews 10:24 of our responsibility in this process to equip and mature fellow Christians with the words, "And let us consider how we may spur (encourage) one another on toward love and good deeds (works)."

James reminds us that faith without works is dead. Strangely, Martin Luther who discovered grace in Paul's letter to new Christians in Rome, considered the Book of James to be a 'book of straw', that is, of little significance. Why of little significance? Luther thought James placed too much emphasis on works. Can a person respond to an altar call and continue to live a self-centered, unchanged life? I've come to the realization that going to church whenever the doors are open is not the same as producing the fruit spoken of by Jesus.

I've never given an altar call in which I didn't invite people to repent of their sins and confess with their mouths and believe (accept in faith) Jesus to be their Lord and Savior. In Romans 10:9-10, Paul said this is what we must do in order to be saved. But, as I read the red words and consider them in light of some current theological beliefs, such as the hyper-grace movement, I am uneasy. Being strongly influenced by my Methodist and Southern Baptist background, I know the doctrine of eternal security as expressed in the words, 'once saved, always saved'. Many sincere, committed and mature Christians are surprised when I tell them these words are not in the bible. This idea is based on our understanding of some red words in John 10:28. Therein Jesus said that no one could take from his hand one of those his Father had given him. Who were they? Were they only his twelve disciples minus Judas, who betrayed Jesus? What about us? There are many other verses of scripture that people point to in support of the 'once saved, always saved' doctrine. Nevertheless, I am concerned - fearing in the absence of a changed life - there may be no true repentance - no real relationship with God through what Jesus did while here on earth 2,000 years ago.

Billy Graham was one of the world's greatest evangelists. I am told that during a PBS interview in the early '90s, Billy Graham stated that he believed that only about twenty-five percent of those who responded to altar calls were actually saved. That is a staggering thought! In the early 1970s many Fundamentalists labeled Billy Graham to be a heretic. They considered his messages to be too simplistic - too elementary. I knew several pastors in the Newport News/Hampton Roads/Norfolk area in 1974 who encouraged their congregations to boycott Billy Graham's Norfolk Crusade.

Not familiar with the term Fundamentalist? Or Fundamentalism? Some of the names associated with Christian Fundamentalism include R. A. Torrey, G. Campbell Morgan, C. I. Schofield (Schofield Bible), B. B. Warfield, and Charles R. Erdman. Fundamentalism developed as a defensive reaction to the teachings of rationalism, liberalism, and higher criticism within the church (more on this shortly). Liberalism began to question the truth - the accuracy of scripture as expressed in the Apostles Creed and the Nicene Creed. The Fundamentalist movement began in the late 19th Century within theological circles and by the 1920s was well established within conservative elements in Christianity. Fundamentalists claimed that scripture was inspired by God, therefore inerrant (without error) - in essence. true from 'In the beginning God' to the last 'Amen' in the book of Revelation. Other foundational beliefs included the virgin birth, the bodily resurrection of Jesus, our justification by Jesus' sinless life and death on the cross, and the belief that Jesus actually performed the miracles spoken of in the Gospels of Matthew, Mark, Luke, and John. To doubt or disbelieve these basic Christian beliefs reduces Christianity to myths and bedtime stories. Many critics of the bible and Christianity deny these fundamental beliefs.

R. A. Torrey, another great world evangelist, worked with D. L. Moody in Chicago and later became the dean of what would become Biola University in California. He was the editor of *The Fundamentals: A Testimony To The Truth*, a collection of 90 essays that addressed concerns related to the issue of divine revelation versus rationalism or a growing trend to question biblical truth and the accuracy of scripture. Known as *The Fundamentals*, this collection of essays, essentially became the foundation of Christian Fundamentalism. Torrey also expressed concerns related to the doctrine of 'once saved, always saved'. He stated that he believed only about ten percent of those who respond to alter calls are actually saved.

C. S. Lewis also expressed concerns regarding the 'once saved, always saved' teaching. It seems to me, since prominent and influential Christian leaders like Martin Luther, Billy Graham, R. A. Torrey, and C. S. Lewis question this doctrinal issue, it may be worthy of our consideration. My thoughts? I believe 'once saved, always saved - **if ever saved**'. The sayings, 'actions speak louder than words' and 'I'd rather see a sermon than hear one' - speak of a changed life. Does NO Change equal NO Salvation?

The title of this book is *Return to Basics: God's Word, The Final Authority*. I think back to the words of A. W. Tozer, who said, "A man of average Intelligence is capable of reading and understanding the bible." The Gospel of Jesus really is simple and elementary.

Do we dare ask probing questions? Dare we step out of our comfort zone? The word dogmatic originates from the Greek word dogma which means, that which one believes to be true. Essentially one who is dogmatic is one who accepts the status quo - often, without question. Such a person tends to be threatened by information that differs from what they've been taught - and accepted as truth. To illustrate this thought, I think back to high school when a Catholic friend told me my Protestant Bible was incomplete. I argued with him until he showed me his bible (proof) and sure enough, his bible contained fourteen more books than my KJV. His bible was complete. WOW! I'd been a Christian for ten years and had never heard the word Apocrypha. Imagine my dismay years later when I discovered the original 1611 KJV was made up of not only the Old Testament and the New Testament but also included the Apocrypha sandwiched between them. The Apocrypha remained in the 1611 KJV until 1885. To this day I've never actually seen a complete 1611 KJV. Theologians, more learned than me question the significance of the Apocrypha. Saint Augustine of Hippo initially believed it should be included in the bible but later in life changed his thoughts somewhat. As I've read the writings of early church fathers I've learned that their thinking was about evenly divided on this issue. Even Martin Luther thought there was value in reading the Apocrypha. While there may be some merit in these books, I believe there is little therein needed for our Christian walk.

In September 1959 I was confronted by a highly respected professor. She was an ordained minister in a major denomination and well-educated having earned a Doctorate in Theology Degree. Her teaching caused me to question what I'd been taught in Sunday school and church. Sadly, she was the product of Julius Wellhausen's religious philosophy known as Higher Criticism. Higher Criticism pitted God's revelation against man's rationalism. Wellhausen was a German professor of religious studies. Higher Criticism questioned whether we could accept the words in the Bible to be true and accurate, to be in fact, *sola scriptura*. *Sola scriptura* (Latin) essentially means 'the only authority within the Church'. Questions raised by higher criticism include: Is it rational to accept divine revelation as truth? Do you personally know of any virgin births? Do you personally know of anyone who was raised from the dead? Or who experienced a 'miraculous' healing. These and many other questions originate from higher criticism. I have known several prominent ministers who doubted some of these beliefs. Can a man or woman in the pulpit doubt the truth of the virgin birth or the bodily resurrection of Jesus and still be an effective leader within the church? My belief is that Christianity stands on the virgin birth and the bodily resurrection of Jesus. If these two events are not fact, then church attendance is a total waste of time and energy. Essentially, liberalism and rationalism replaced our trust in God's words revealed in the Bible. Rationalism versus revelation became the issue in seminaries on the East Coast of America during the early 1900s.

To learn more about the issue of higher criticism you might want to read *7 MEN WHO RULE THE WORLD FROM THE GRAVE*, written by Dave W. Breese and published in 1990. The men named in his book are: Charles Darwin, Karl Marx, Julius Wellhausen, John Dewey, Sigmund Freud, John Maynard Keynes, and Soren Kierkegaard. Breese also mentions an eighth man, Albert Einstein. Each of these men was and is in the truest sense, a mover and shaker. These men and their thoughts continue to have tremendous influence in all areas of our world in 2021. While each of these men is highly regarded, have you ever considered the impact their lives and thoughts have on you and your thinking? Several of these men had backgrounds in theology or were raised in Jewish families. I've pondered life as we know it in the 21st Century and often asked the question, what went wrong? Breese's book helps answer this and several other related questions.

An aside: are you familiar with the word WELTAN-SCHAUUNG? This German word is the combination of two words: *welt* (world) and *anschauung* (view). Combined, the word is defined as worldview. Our worldview influences how we live our lives and how we interact with others and to a large degree, what we consider to be right or wrong, or the norm. Essentially our worldview largely determines how we live. Several examples of worldview are Buddhism, Hinduism, Islam, Judaism, Christianity, Socialism, Marxism, and Communism, just to name a few. Years ago I wrote a paper in which I responded to a Christian missionary who was married to a card-carrying Communist. He essentially believed you could be both a Christian and a Communist. I pointed out to this missionary that Christianity and Communism were mutually exclusive. Both share a similar belief. That belief? Thou shall have no other God before me. One of the men in Breese's book, Karl Marx, is the father of Marxism. I believe Socialism and Communism are fruit from the tree of Marxism.

The world population is approaching 7.6 billion. About 1.6 billion people in the world are Muslims who follow the teachings of Mohammed. Their worldview is known as Islam. The word

Islam is defined as 'submission'. The word Muslim is defined as 'one who submits'. Islam is one of the fastest-growing religions today, especially in our prison systems. The difference between Islam and any other religion or worldview is the ultimate objective of Islam. The objective for Islam and Muslims? The entire world united under Islam and its Sharia law - no more parliamentary or constitutional law or law as you know it. The term for this condition is Dar al-Islam. In the Islamic world Christians, Jews, and all others who are not Muslims are identified as infidels. I find it incomprehensible that Dave Breese did not include Mohammed in his list of men who rule the world from the grave. Breese's book was published in 1990. And yet, C. S. Lewis expressed concerns about Islam in his book, *Mere Christianity* which was first published in 1943. Think about the Tower of Babel and God's reaction to a world united.

The heading for this chapter: **Savior? or Lord and Savior?** I believe scripture is very clear regarding the choice to obey or disobey what God tells us to do. Can Jesus be your Savior if He is not also Lord of your life? Am I a heretic for asking this question? What is heresy? Simply stated, heresy is any belief contrary to beliefs held by the majority of any group; in this case Christians. And a heretic? One who holds that different belief. What of once saved always saved? See Chapter 6.

CHAPTER 6
SIGNS OF DISCIPLESHIP/ RELATIONSHIP?

Do you seek to rightly divide God's word? What is the purpose of rightly dividing God's word? I suggest the purpose is that we become Christlike. Where do you begin? Hopefully you begin with Bible in hand. Which version do you read or study? Is it the KJV, or the RSV, or the NIV, or the NAS, or the ESV or any of the alternatives? There are even parallel bibles with several side-by-side versions enabling you to read and compare different versions of the Bible. Then we have cultural study bibles which provide insight into the customs and traditions of the people spoken of in God's word. In addition, there are countless resources available to help study God's word. There are concordances and exhaustive concordances. There are bible dictionaries. And Greek and Hebrew word studies. Then we have a vast number of bible commentaries. All of these resources have one thing in common: the authors were and are scholars who have devoted their lives to 'rightly dividing God's word'. And yet, there are subtle differences in their understanding of God's word. How we live our life as a Christian is determined by our understanding of God's word.

When the Apostle Paul wrote to the early Churches he told new Christians how they should act and what they should look like. He told them a two-faceted truth: positional truth (who they are in and through the works of Jesus) and temporal or practical truth (how they should live). Volumes have been written by bible scholars expounding on these issues. Scholars define and discuss countless theological concepts: grace, mercy, salvation, justification, redemption, predestination, different types of love, adoption, and transformation just to name a few. There are books written on each of these words. Are there consequences when we fail to grasp the meanings of words in God's word? If I understand the intent of scripture, it is that we are to be transformed (changed) by God's words. How about the words obedience and submission?

The New Testament was written by several authors guided by God, and is about Jesus, his disciples, his Church, and ends with the book of Revelation. Essentially, the New Testament is the unfolding of God's plan begun way, way back at the beginning of time with the words, 'In the beginning God'. The life of Jesus is prophesied several hundred times in the Old Testament. Jesus is the central figure throughout the New Testament. Ultimately the Bible is about Jesus, and what he did and said, what we as Christ followers should be doing and where we will spend eternity. It is not my intention to cause anyone to doubt their salvation. But, having given and witnessed many altar calls and subsequent confessions of faith and baptisms I am left with a nagging question. The question? What happened afterwards? In the absence of a changed life I, like Martin Luther, R. A. Torrey, Billy Graham and C. S. Lewis have cause to wonder about those who responded to an altar call - and then disappeared from view. Was it an emotional flash during a moment of personal crisis and did the cares of the world then overwhelm them? Were they not discipled or mentored in sound biblical principles. Were they not lifted up in prayer by the church? Were they left to fend for themselves? Did they not feel welcome and accepted? Were good seeds planted by the pastor during the sermon?

Jesus' parable of the sower and the seeds in Matthew 13 speaks of four different scenarios. Some seeds were sown along a path and were eaten by birds. Other seeds were sown in rocky places and didn't grow. Other seeds were choked out by thorns (the problems of life?). Only the seeds sown in fertile ground took root and then produced a good crop - some a 100 fold, others 60 fold or 30 fold - but they all produced. I find it interesting that only 25 percent of the seeds mentioned in this parable survived to produce a crop. Those in church leadership and we as Christians have an obligation to follow up with people who take that initial leap of faith. Only God knows the answer to the question, who is and who isn't? IS and ISN'T? Saved! The intention of this chapter is that any one reading these words examine their life in light of God's Word.

What did Jesus and the writers of the New Testament say about obedience and submission? Jesus said some tough things during his time on earth as did others who wrote portions of the New Testament. My prayer is that I not take the text out of context. There is a severe warning spoken by Paul to those who pervert (add to or take away from) the Gospel of Jesus Christ. That severe warning is also spoken of in Revelation 22.

The Book of Revelation is the last book of the New Testament. Revelation focuses on the study of eschatology (what will take place in the end times). It may be that Revelation is the least understood book in either the Old Testament or the New Testament. Chapters 2 and 3 are written to seven churches located in Asia Minor. Those churches? Ephesus, Smyrna, Pergamum, Thyatira, Sardis, Philadelphia and Laodicea. Jesus first compliments each of them. Jesus then identifies issues within these churches. Issues? Ephesus: you've left your first love. Smyrna: be faithful even to the point of death. Pergamum: you have people who heed the teachings of Balaam and are sexually immoral. Thyatira: you tolerate Jezebel and sexual immorality. Sardis: you are dead - wake up. Philadelphia: hold onto what you have, so no one can take your crown. Laodicea: you are lukewarm and rich - but are wretched, poor, blind and naked. A dire consequence for this church and their lukewarm condition? Jesus says because you are lukewarm I will spit you out of my mouth.

Is it okay to be hot or cold but not lukewarm? What is the danger in being lukewarm? Could it be the definition of lukewarm is that we are just 'going through the motions' - 'just showing up at church on the occasional Sunday' or hoping 'we can fake it, til we make it' or thinking 'my brother or father or uncle was a pastor or deacon'? In Christianity there are no 'coat tails' we can hang onto - coat tails will not get us into Heaven. It's all about a personal choice! Remember, Christianity is a personal relationship. Were these warnings written only to those seven churches? Or do they also apply to you and me? What about todays pulpits which are silent about abortion, or alternative lifestyles or social issues? Jesus challenges each of these seven churches to be victorious - to be over comers. For each of these churches there were rewards and consequences for their actions as there will be for us today.

Over time God has established different types of treaties or covenants with his people. Some of these covenants were unconditional, others conditional. A covenant between a king or ruler and his subjects was known as a suzerain-vassal covenant - a conditional covenant. It seems the words spoken to these seven churches was such a covenant. What is the church? Again, His Church is you and me bought and paid for with His innocent blood. Let me be absolutely clear, there is no salvation, no life eternal in heaven with God except on the basis of the innocent blood shed by Jesus. Jesus went to the cross out of obedience and submission to God. That Jesus died to redeem us from death and sin is the central theme of the New Testament. Works are not a key to unlock Heaven's door or a condition to receive salvation! But, how important are works? Are they evidence of a changed life?

It is my conviction there are a couple of other key words in the New Testament which should influence how we as Christians live. One of them is Lord. The word Lord might be understood to be a simple term of respect, as in Sir. The word had a deeper meaning. People who heard Jesus speak understood the meaning of this word. One who was a lord was lord over something - a kingdom ruled over but occupied by people. Think owner, master, authority figure or one to whom allegiance or loyalty is due. Potentially, a lord had the power of life and death over his servants, slaves or subjects. Hence, to disobey the commands of a lord was to risk punishment, perhaps even death. Our altar calls **ALWAYS** invite a person to accept Jesus as Lord **and** Savior. Do we understand the implications therein? There is an unpopular term, Lordship Salvation (considered by many in the church to be heresy) which states that unless Jesus is Lord of our lives, then he is not our Savior. Why do we invite people to accept Jesus as both Lord and Savior? **If not Lord, why not simply invite people to accept Jesus as Savior?**

A second key word is disciple. This word was frequently used in the Gospels. When the word disciple was used it had a common meaning. A true disciple was obedient to, committed to, surrendered to, and transformed by the teachings of the master or teacher. Transformed? Scripture (Romans) tells us we are to be 'transformed by the renewing of our minds'. We are also told to 'let the word/mind/peace of Christ dwell richly in us'. A disciple was expected to become a duplicate of the master. What a disciple said and did - his life was to be a copy of the master's life. The disciples of Jesus were obedient and faithful to the command he gave them in Matthew 28. The life they lived - their actions testified to the fact they were truly disciples of Christ. Many were persecuted and died because they were obedient to his commands - that they were true disciples. Do these thoughts challenge us today? Do you and I look like Jesus?

Jesus teaches a parable in Matthew 13 regarding wheat and tares (weeds) growing in a farmers field. In this parable we are told the farmer planted wheat seeds and that an enemy then planted tare seeds in the farmer's field. Countless sermons have been preached on this parable. Many equate this story to the church. Essentially a tare, as it grows along side wheat, looks like the real thing. However, only at harvest time is the difference apparent. When ready for harvest a head of wheat droops or hangs over while the head of a tare continues to stand straight up. Is there a comparison therein with the church in 2021? My fear is that many in today's church will hear the words of Jesus words spoken in Matthew 7:21-23, which essentially say, 'Depart from me for I never knew you because you weren't about my Father's kingdom business.' Or expressed a little differently, 'you were going through the motions, but we had no relationship'. The destination for tares? Jesus said at harvest time they would be gathered up and tossed into the fire? Are you wheat or tares? What is your destination? Eternity is a really long time!

Christianity essentially has to do with a changed relationship. If we are Christians we are no longer enemies of God - no longer outsiders - no longer Gentiles. We are now related to God through what Jesus did while he ministered here on earth. We are also related to other Christians as in, we are now part of the family of God. As family we have the responsibility to love one another - to pray for others - to bear each other's burdens - to help when and where help is needed - to think more highly of others than we do of ourselves - to encourage and set an example for our church family - in essence, to be salt and light. Remember the saying on that church marquee? **Christianity is not a religion, but a relationship.**

Another significant word was used only by Paul in the New Testament. It is the word adoption which he used five times in his letters. Most of what follows is the result of research done in a Catholic University library while pursuing a degree in Criminal Justice Management and pre-law. The Greek word for adoption is huiothesia and has its origin in the Greek/Roman legal system. **NOTE:** the adopted child was not necessarily a minor; i.e. age was not a factor. Some of the legal highlights of the word adoption follow. The adoptive father initiated the adoption procedure and the adopted child had the choice to respond or not respond. Debts owed by the adopted child were paid by the father. The father had the right to control the behavior of the child, including who the child associated with and how the child spent his time. The father had the right to discipline the child. The child's possessions became the father's possessions. Both the adoptive father and the adopted child were committed to each other. Perhaps the most striking feature in the process of adoption is that once entered into, the adoption could not be challenged by any legal process. I believe Paul's use of the word huiothesia reveals Paul's deep insight into the relationship brought about by the salvation experience. God the Father, initiated our adoption into his family through the actions of God the Son (Jesus) who canceled our debt. Our adoption begins when we respond to an altar call for salvation and confess Jesus to be our Savior - but is that all there is? Have you truly been adopted into God's family or are you 'just going through the motions'?

When Mom divorced my paternal father and married Pop, he adopted me and changed my name - think legal stuff. When Pop did these things he accepted a legal responsibility for me. He was expected to provide me with the essentials of life - food, clothing, shelter, medical care, and an education. I being adopted, had responsibilities to Pop - to obey him and to submit to him. If I chose to disobey Pop, he had the right to discipline me. Did he discipline me because he didn't like me? No! He did so out of love and concern for me - as in, 'train up a child'. Paul essentially says that God adopts us into his family based on the life and works of Jesus. Scripture tells us we are saved by grace and not by our personal efforts (works). A simple definition of grace is God's unmerited favor - it is a God given gift, not something we've earned by anything we've done. Grace is something originating with God - an outpouring of God's love - the essence of who God is. Scripture (John 3:16) tells us that God's desire is that no one perish but that all have life everlasting. Jesus was, is, and always will be God's Plan A. I can not do anything in and of myself to earn this thing called salvation. Salvation is however, a personal choice. That choice? To accept Jesus Christ as both Lord and Savior?

What is the significance of works in the life of a Christian? I'll go back to a single verse of scripture in the Old Testament book of 1 Samuel 15:22 in which God tells us 'to obey is better than sacrifice'. Remember that God does not change. Jesus said, "I and my Father are one". The following verses of scripture are from Matthew, Luke, John, Acts, Hebrews, James, 1 John and Revelation. Nearly two thousand years have passed since these gospels and letters were written. The selected verses address the twin issues of obedience and submission.

Remember the red words? Jesus began his earthly ministry with the same words spoken by John the Baptist. Jesus and John spoke of the kingdom of heaven and repentance (to turn from our wicked ways). Why repent? Because the kingdom of heaven is at hand. Jesus called people to repent, to change, and produce works which would be a living testimony of their actual repentance - to live a changed life. Jesus says in Matthew 7:21 "Not everyone who says to me Lord, Lord will enter the kingdom of heaven but only he who does the will of my Father who is in heaven." This same message is also recorded in Luke 6:46 "Why do you call me Lord, Lord, and do not do what I say?" The obvious message is that calling Jesus Lord and then not doing what Jesus tells us to do is an act of disobedience. He then says in Matthew 14:50 "For whoever does the will of my Father in heaven is my brother and sister and mother." Herein, Jesus is speaking of relationship. Remember, part of the Great Commission given by Jesus in Matthew 28:18-21 includes the words, "All authority in heaven and earth has been given to me. Therefore go and make disciples … teaching them to obey everything I have commanded you." The words OBEY and COMMAND seem to be of significance to Jesus.

In our Christian walk we endeavor to seek the truth - to separate fact from fiction. John 8:31-32 states, "... if you hold to my teaching you are really my disciples. Then you will know the truth, and the truth will set you free." In this same Gospel (John 14 and 15) Jesus repeatedly (10 times) stresses the importance of OBEYING, of DOING, and of BEARING FRUIT. You might think of these words as evidence of repentance and a changed life. Luke in Acts 5:32 states, "... the Holy Spirit whom God has given, to those who obey him." There's that word again - OBEY. Is receiving the Holy Spirit conditioned upon our obedience to God? Does this mean if we don't obey, we don't receive the Holy Spirit? There are those among us who believe the Holy Spirit is received by all when they respond to an altar call and make a confession of faith. Others believe that receiving the Holy Spirit is a second occurrence subsequent to a confession of faith. There's that division again!

The writer of Hebrews also thought obedience was important. Hebrews 5:8-9 states, "Although he was a son, he learned obedience from what he suffered, and, once made perfect he became the source of eternal salvation for all who obey him." Think about the implications therein! Had Jesus failed to obey God there would be no salvation for us. James 1:22 warns, "Do not merely listen to the word, and so deceive yourselves. Do what it says." Chapter 2:3-6 of 1 John tells us, "We know that we have come to know him if we obey his commands. The man who says I know him, but does not do what he commands is a liar, and the truth is not in him. But if anyone obeys his word, God's love is truly made complete in him. Whoever claims to live in him must walk as Jesus did." The importance of obeying is further stressed in 1 John 3:24, with the words, "Those who obey his commands, live in him."

There are books written which include the words, "Purpose Driven" this or that. Existentialism attempts to answer the questions of "why do I exist? - "what is the purpose of my life"? Go back to the book of Revelation. Revelation 1:5 has the words, "To him (Jesus) who loves us and has freed us from our sins by his blood, and has made us to be a kingdom and priests to serve his God and Father." Have you ever considered yourself to be part of a kingdom? AND to be a priest within that kingdom? AND that you exist and your purpose in life is to serve God! Are you doing that?

What of the words in Revelation 22:14? The King James Version states, "Blessed are they who do his commandments, that they may have right to the tree of life, and may enter in through the gates of the city." If the King James Version is correct, the obvious conclusion is that those who do not do his commandments will not have the right to the tree of life and will not enter through the gates of the city. Several other bible versions have an alternate interpretation of this passage substituting the words, "Blessed are those who wash their robes." Wash their robes? Obvious conclusion? With the blood of the Lamb which washes our sins away. What Jesus did while here on earth makes us acceptable to God. His obedience plus God's grace imparts righteousness and holiness to us. Regardless of the bible you study, scripture does seem to emphasize the importance of obedience and submission throughout God's word.

The importance of obedience and the consequences for disobedience to God's commands, for individuals as well as collectively for God's people, are stressed throughout God's word. Think of these promises as an IF/THEN proposition. Deuteronomy 28 is very clear about the choice to obey or to disobey. It promises blessings for obedience or curses for disobedience. Verse 13 states, "The Lord will make you the head, not the tail. If you pay attention to the commands of the Lord your God that I give you this day and carefully follow them you will always be at the top, never at the bottom." The consequences for failure to follow God's commands are then spelled out in Verses 43 and 44 which warn, "The alien who lives among you will rise above you higher and higher, but you will sink lower and lower. He will lend to you, but you will not lend to him. He will be the head, but you will be the tail." These words were written about 3,500 years ago. Were these words written, only to the Israelites? Do you think these warnings have any relevance for Christians today or for our nation in the early 21st century? I guess it depends on your mindset. Are you a New Testament ONLY Christian? Remember the words of Saint Augustine of Hippo. "The new (testament) is in the old contained; the old (testament) is by the new explained." Or to put it differently, 'scripture interprets scripture'.

There are many words in the New Testament which tell us as Christians what we should be doing - what we should look like. These words tell us who we are in and through the life that Jesus lived during his earthly ministry. Have you ever said to yourself, 'I'm not a preacher'. And yet, what you do and say has eternal consequences. We, you and me, may be the only Jesus many people will ever see. Our life is a living testimony (sermon). Is my life a sermon that will bring lost people to a relationship with God through his son, Jesus?

Many of the words Jesus spoke - doing, bearing fruit, obeying and disobeying are action verbs - requiring a response. The question we all should ask and answer today is the same question Jesus asked 2,000 years ago. That question? **"Why do you call me Lord, Lord and don't do what I've told you?"**

CHAPTER 7

DOCTRINE? - NECESSARY? (IF SO, WHICH?)

Questions, questions, questions - where do we begin? A simple definition of doctrine is the guiding beliefs held in common within a denomination. Doctrine has to do with what we do and why we do the things we do in church. Doctrinal beliefs should be based on scripture rather than the traditions of men. And ultimately, if we truly believe scripture, then the life we live should be guided by and changed by what we profess to be true. Going back to the saying on that church marquee I mentioned in the introduction. It said, **"You only believe that part of scripture that you do. All else is just idle talk."** The study of doctrine tends to be somewhat unpopular, even the source of division in today's churches (identified in scripture as, the body of Christ). In defense of his doctrinal beliefs, a sincere but dogmatic friend recently stated, "You've got to know what you believe or you'll fall for anything." I suggest it's the WHO YOU BELIVE IN, coupled with what you believe that is the key issue. I believe it is possible to be **sincerely** wrong in what we believe - especially if you're the **I** in the word sincerely.

In September 1959, at the age of seventeen I entered a pre-ministerial course of study at a Christian college. An assignment required that students research and identify the doctrinal beliefs of major Christian denominations in the local area. It surprised me to learn that approximately eighty-five percent of Christian beliefs are held in common. Only fifteen percent of our beliefs divide us. Issues such as the form of baptism: do you sprinkle or immerse or baptize infants or is baptism really necessary for salvation are such issues. Or does your church baptize only in the name of Jesus rather than in the name of the Father, Son and Holy Spirit as Jesus instructed in Mathew 28? Is your denomination Calvinistic, believing that God pre-selected those who would be saved (predestination)? If so, the rest of us are doomed to an eternity in hell. Or is your denomination Arminian, believing that we are free agents having the freedom to choose to be saved by God's grace? Or does your denomination combine elements of both doctrines? Does your denomination believe in Replacement Theology - that the Church has replaced Israel in God's ultimate plan? Or ordain women as church leaders? Are women only fit to teach Children's Sunday School classes, mind the nursery, or sing in the choir? What about church leaders who practice an alternative lifestyle? Is your denomination King James Only? Is the observance of The Lord's Supper/Communion OPEN (available to any who profess Jesus as savior) or CLOSED (available only to members of that local church body)? Related to The Lord's Supper/Communion, does your denomination believe the doctrine of transubstantiation which claims the bread and wine actually become the body and blood of Jesus when consumed?. Do you practice foot washings?

Are women allowed to wear slacks/trousers or are they expected to wear dresses? Do we omit the use of musical instruments and sing *a cappella* in our worship services? Does your church service begin with some form of creedal statement such as the Apostles' or Nicene Creed? What about the creedal statement, "No Creed But Christ, No Book But The Bible"? Division versus Unity. In John 17:20-23 Jesus prays to his Father that his disciples (his followers-you and me?) may be one, as he and his Father are one. Jesus is praying for unity within his body - within his Church. Again, it's HIS CHURCH! He's the Bridegroom and we (the Church) are his Bride.

Admittedly, my theological beliefs have been influenced by my years in the Methodist, Baptist and other denominations during my sixty plus year search to understand God's word. Hence, I am not a *tabula rasa*; the Latin term for a blank slate. In other words, I was not raised in a Christian vacuum (single denomination). Or you can use the word eclectic to describe my theology - a theology based upon broad or diverse Christian teachings.

Methodist vs Baptist? Years ago when friends questioned the difference between the two, my somewhat glib response was Methodists can dance and play cards but Baptists can't do either (I was a Methodist). That distinction is long gone. Baptist? More than 60 flavors of Baptist, hence we are even divided within our denominations. I believe most church members today would be hard pressed to state the doctrines of the church they attend.

What is your denominational predisposition. Do you know the doctrinal beliefs of the church you attend? Are they based on God's revealed word or are they based on the traditions of men? Are you like the Bereans mentioned in Acts 17 who were diligent (they searched the scriptures) in their study of God's word? Paul the apostle, wrote a letter to his protege Timothy and encouraged him to study (the scriptures) to show (prove) himself to be a workman who correctly and accurately presented God's word to those he taught (preached to). I think more accurately, Paul encouraged that Timothy's life be a living example (above reproach) to those to whom Timothy ministered - that he walk the walk and not merely talk the talk. Timothy was not a casual observer. He was stoned to death for his commitment to the Gospel of Jesus Christ. Occasionally I hear a sermon in which scripture is twisted to support some personal point of view. Or expressed differently, the text is taken out of context. Do you search God's word for the truth therein? Or are we preoccupied with other stuff - our priorities over God's priorities?

The bookcases within pastors' studies often are lined with volumes of expensive books - pretty impressive. Therein you'll find concordances, commentaries, word studies - both Greek and Hebrew, expository dictionaries, the writings of early church fathers, historical and cultural studies which provide details of the people spoken of in the bible. The books within a pastor's study reveal a great deal about a pastor's beliefs. The list of resources goes on and on. These references ultimately provide a wealth of information, sometimes used by pastors in the preparation of their eloquent sermons and teachings. These impressive references cost thousands of dollars. E. M. Bounds in his book *Power Thru Prayer* stated, "Colleges, learning, books, theology, preaching cannot make a preacher, but praying does." My extensive collection of books did not make me a better husband, father, neighbor, or Christian. Eventually, I took a truck load of those expensive books to a Christian book store to be recycled. I'm still working on the praying part!

In reality the books which have made the greatest impact on my life are the writings of Christians who wrote of their personal experiences with God and his Son, who is the author and finisher of my still, flawed life. The books I read are very personal in that I use both a highlighter and a pen as I read. They are filled with intimate comments about my life experiences as I read and reflected on the printed words therein. For that reason some of these books are never loaned to anyone! What follows are some of my favorite authors and books which I recommend.

One such author was Aiden Wilson Tozer born in the late 19th Century. Tozer did not graduate from high school. He received no formal theological training. And yet, he received honorary doctoral degrees from Wheaton and Houghton colleges. Tozer was the editor of *The Alliance Weekly* magazine. He was also a prolific author and influential pastor, his ministry spanning more than four decades. I highly recommend three of his books, *The Knowledge of the Holy*, *The Pursuit of God*, and *God's Pursuit of Man* which are available in a single volume. Going back to the words of Tozer, he said a person of average intelligence can read and understand God's word. It is recorded that Tozer devoted about three hours of his day to prayer - time alone with God. Tozer's ministry was dedicated to helping people enter into a personal relationship with God. He was also concerned about the direction and future of the church..

A contemporary of A. W. Tozer was C. S. Lewis, who wrote *Mere Christianity*, one of my all time favorites. Both C. S. Lewis and A. W. Tozer, were prolific writers who died within 6 months of each other in 1963.

Other authors at the top of my list include Dietrich Bonhoeffer and his book, *The Cost of Discipleship*. Arthur W. Pink, also a contemporary of Tozer and Lewis, wrote *The Sovereignty of God*. A more recent author was Brennan Manning and his books, *Abba's Child*, *The Ragamuffin Gospel*, and *The Relentless Tenderness of Jesus*.

Erwin W. Lutzer wrote *Hitler's Cross*, a disturbing insight into the church's failure to act in the face of evil. My wife, Kathy, often says I only read heavy books. A great book, especially for those interested in Christian apologetics (essentially a defense of why we can trust the accuracy of God's word) is the updated, *Evidence That Demands A Verdict*, co-authored by Josh McDowell and his son, Sean McDowell, PhD. J. Dwight Pentecost was a Professor of Bible Exposition, Emeritus at Dallas Theological Seminary (DTS). Two of his books, *Things To Come*, and *Things Which Become Sound Doctrine: Doctrinal Studies of Fourteen Crucial Words of Faith* are heavy books. A virtual 'Who's Who' of other Christian leaders associated with DTS include: J. Vernon McGee, Charles Ryrie, Lewis S. Chafer, John W. Walvoord, Chuck Swindoll, Tony Evans, Robert Jeffress, and David Jeremiah, just to name a few.

Pausing for a moment, I want to quote from the words of Dietrich Bonhoeffer - words which seem particularly appropriate in our deeply troubled and divided nation. Bonhoeffer was an outspoken Lutheran pastor who was imprisoned and executed in a German concentration camp during World War II. Executed? Why? Because he was implicated in a plot to assassinate Adolph Hitler. Bonhoeffer was critical of the church because it failed to speak out against the atrocities committed against the Jews. He was speaking of this evil when he said, **"Silence in the face of evil, is itself evil: God will not hold us guiltless. Not to speak is to speak. Not to act is to act."** Is there a message therein for the church today?

Martin Niemoller was also a Lutheran pastor in Nazi Germany. Niemoller initially supported Hitler's 'Final Solution' to deal with the Jews in Germany, but after being sent to two German concentration camps he wrote a poem. While a couple of versions of his poem exist, they all express the same sentiments. Essentially he said they came for the communists, then for the socialists, then for the trade unionists, then for the Jews - but I wasn't one of them. Then they came for me and no one was left to defend me. **It seems we're okay when it's them, but not okay when it's me.** Is life all about me, my, and mine?

On that thought, Erwin W. Lutzer's book *Hitler's Cross,* tells of a church in Nazi Germany, behind which was a railroad. In the dead of winter, each Sunday morning while the church met, the congregation would hear the cries of Jews who were packed into unheated boxcars like cattle - boxcars with no sanitary facilities - as the train passed behind the church. The Jews were on the way to their deaths in the concentration camps. How did that church respond to those desperate cries as they sat in the warmth and comfort of their church building? They turned up the volume and sang their hymns (worshipping God) louder to drown out the desperate cries of the men, women and children - six million innocent victims of Hitler's 'Final Solution' - victims of the Holocaust. Hitler's 'Final Solution' targeted not only the Jews, but also gays, the mentally challenged, and Christians. Why were Christians silent? Did they fear persecution if they opposed Hitler's Final Solution? Were they truly Christians? Could something like the Holocaust happen again? How about the ethnic cleansing, which includes Christians, in several African countries?

I occasionally hear the term 'consumer-friendly' used to describe 21st Century churches. Are we truly, so 'heavenly minded that we're no earthly good'? Why has the church at large been silent on social issues? Issues like abortion and racism, both of which devalue life - life of the inconvenient unborn and people of color. A reminder: Adam and Eve were created in God's image. How about the homeless, the poor and the hungry? If we're Christians, are we truly Christ followers and if we are, is something more required of us? In addressing some of these issues we are inclined to use the words of Jesus to justify our indifference to those less fortunate than us. It may be that we occasionally take the text (scripture) out of context. Exegesis, hermeneutics, and the law of first mention, all have to do with the interpretation of scripture and our understanding thereof.

The word poor, also linked to poverty, is used in both the Old and New Testaments. I occasionally hear Christians justify their lack of concern for the needy with these words, "Well Jesus said, we'll always have the poor among us." Did he really say this? Or did he say, "The poor you will always have with you, but you will not always have me." Read Matthew 26:11 and John 12:8 and you'll find that Jesus was rebuking some of his listeners, rather than condemning the poor to a life of poverty. Mark 14:7 says, "The poor you will always have with you, and you can help them any time you want. But you will not always have me." Regardless of which version of God's word you read it is obvious that we are to help the poor. How about the Beatitudes? The words of Jesus in Luke 6:20 say, "Blessed are you who are poor, for yours is the kingdom of God." Matthew 5:3 gives a little different perspective of Jesus' words. It says, "Blessed are the poor in spirit for theirs is the kingdom of heaven."

I may be taking liberty with God's word, but Luke 6:24 speaks to the rich with these words, "But woe to you who are rich for you have already received your reward." Poor versus Rich? The words of Jesus in three of the gospels, Matthew 19, Mark 10 and Luke 18, give the account of a self-righteous rich man who claimed to have kept all of the commandments from his birth. Jesus challenged him to sell all that he had and give it to the poor and then follow Jesus. The man walked away, sadly because he was very wealthy.

Jesus used another parable in Luke 18 - a parable comparing the attitude of a self righteous Jewish leader (a Pharisee) and a tax collector (hated among the Jews) both of whom were at the temple to pray. Pharisees were inclined to look down on everyone who was not a Pharisee. The Pharisee thanked God that he was not like other men - robbers, evildoers, adulterers and even this tax collector. He even had the audacity to remind God that he fasted twice a week and tithed a tenth of all he made. In contrast, the tax collector would not even look toward heaven - he beat his breast and said, "God have mercy on me, a sinner." It may be there is a message for us today. Perhaps we should remember, 'except for the grace of God, there go I.'

It may be that 'poor in spirit' is closely akin to the word meek. Meekness may be that state of mind which acknowledges that there is nothing I can do to be worthy of or earn salvation and that I am dead in my trespasses (sin) - the realization that I am spiritually bankrupt - that there is nothing good in me. My only hope comes through the virgin birth of Jesus, his sinless life, his crucifixion, his shed blood and his resurrection to sit at the right hand of his father, God - a place of supreme honor. Only what Jesus did while on earth, combined with your personal decision to accept Jesus as both Lord and Savior, and the life you live thereafter have any significance in the grand scheme of things. I'm convinced the only things in life that matter are those things that have eternal consequences - all else is fluff.

Oh yeah! New Testament versus Old Testament? The word poor and related words such as poverty, oppression of the poor and the concept of justice are intertwined throughout all of scripture, both Old and New. An aside: did you know there was more than one tithe in the Old Testament? One of those tithes given every three years was God's provision for the poor (see Deuteronomy 14:28-29). Can you imagine the reaction if your pastor added another tithe on top of the tithe at your church? There are hundreds of scripture verses addressing these issues. It's pretty clear that God cares for the poor. Thirty-two years ago Kathy and I attended a church in which a deacon cast a deciding vote on an issue related to helping recovering alcoholics and also, young, unwed mothers in the local community who needed to learn life skills (they simply needed a meeting place). This church leader did so with the remark, "Let them pull themselves up by their bootstraps. I never had to do anything for my kids and they turned out okay." I think he had not read Proverbs 14:31 which states, "Whoever oppresses (doesn't help/treats with contempt) the poor shows contempt for their Maker (God their creator), but whoever is kind to the needy honors God." When we honor God with our actions is that the same as 'worshipping God in spirit and in truth'? The active membership of that church today numbers only four. They do however still have a really nice building which they call church.

I left an author and one his books out of my list of Christian authors and significant books. Bill Hybels wrote a book which challenges Christians to be the hands and feet of Jesus. The book published in 2004, is titled, *The Volunteer REVOLUTION: Unleashing the Power of Everybody.* I believe there is in God's word, something of a social gospel established by the Golden Rule - remember, "Do unto others". To their credit, there are many Christian groups actively involved in volunteer activities, e.g. Samaritan's Purse, Operation Christmas Child (the shoebox ministry), Operation Blessing, various area rescue ministries, the Southern Baptist Disaster Relief effort, Family Promise and The Salvation Army, just to name a few. As Christ followers we should be in the forefront of reaching out to people in times of need.

Sadly, many in the Christian community perceive the term social gospel in a negative sense and taken to its extreme, I believe it can be, in fact, quite negative. Lest I be labeled one who believes in some form of radical, liberal, left-wing, social gospel which espouses free everything - housing, education, medical care and handouts for everyone, please consider the following verse of scripture. 2 Thessalonians 3:10-12 states that a man who won't work shouldn't be fed. Old Testament versus New Testament? The book of Proverbs is considered to be a book of wisdom. Check out Proverbs 10:4 which states, "Lazy hands make for poverty, but diligent hands bring wealth." Proverbs 20:13 and 21:17 also express similar thoughts.

If you've read this far it wasn't out of idle curiosity. As I've stated before, God is not a serendipity kinda guy. God doesn't change from day to day - he doesn't react to changing circumstances. It's kinda, 'His way or the highway'. In Deuteronomy 15:11 God reveals to us how we should treat the poor. "There will always be poor people in the land. Therefore I command you to be openhanded (generous) toward your fellow Israelites who are poor and needy in your land." Israelites? Why that's Old Testament!!! If your mindset is that you are a New Testament believer and that the Old Testament no longer applies to you and your life - sorry. If you truly believe that, why do you bother to memorize the Ten Commandments or the 23rd Psalm? Or for that matter claim 2 Chronicles 7:14 which is God's promise to Israel stating, "If my people who are called by my name, will humble themselves and pray and seek my face and turn from their wicked ways, then I will hear from heaven and I will forgive their sin and I will heal their land." You might want to read verse 13 and the remainder of 2 Chronicles chapter 7. Therein you'll find the consequences for a nation which turns away from God - but then, most of us only want to hear the 'good promises'. Remember suzerain-vassal treaties from Chapter 6? They were treaties between a sovereign being and his subjects. Such treaties were conditioned upon the terms, **I will do this, if you do this**. The Old Testament is a transition to the New Testament and raises the bar. God's word (the Bible) is a promise book, beginning with Genesis and ending with Revelation. BIBLE? I've heard it referred to as: Basic Instructions Before Leaving Earth.

Hmmmm! Just a reminder, God gave the Ten to Moses - Jewish religious leaders embellished the Ten to Six Hundred Thirteen. In the Gospels of Matthew, Mark and Luke Jesus reduces the commandments to just two: love God and your fellow man. Then in Galatians 5:14, God speaking through Paul, reduces the commands to a single command: Love your neighbor. Another reminder: Tozer said, "A man of average intelligence can read and understand God's word." It really is simple stuff - really basic. Maybe it's time we RETURN TO BASICS!

So? What about doctrine? Did you expect me to give you a list of necessary doctrines? Sorry, I'm not God! Philippians 2:12 ends with Paul's admonition to "… continue to work out your salvation with fear and trembling …" In other words, 'it ain't over til it's over'. I think a good beginning is The Apostles' Creed or the Nicene Creed. I also think Baptism and The Lord's Supper (Communion) should be included. And we should be driven by the life and teachings of Jesus and the principles and precepts from Genesis through Revelation. Will we ever fully understand every minute point therein? Do we need to? NO! But if we are serious about being Christ followers we must seek to be doers rather than just hearers and talkers. Our priorities should be driven by God's priorities. What does that look like? Ultimately, it begins and ends with loving one another as God loves us. See John 3:16 for clarification.

The New Testament tells us (Christians) that we are no longer strangers. no longer aliens, no longer Gentiles (people without hope). Instead, we're branches which have been grafted into the vine. We've been adopted into God's family. Family is about relationship. Pop's last words to me, in the form of a question, continue to haunt me thirty-four years after he spoke them. That question? "Why did you hate me?" A time will come when each of us stands before the author of creation - Father God. Will we hear the words, "Well done, thou good and faithful servant." Or will we hear the words, "Depart from me for I never knew you." Ultimately it's all about the choices we make in life. Some choices do have everlasting (eternal) consequences.

Isn't it time that we act like family and be about Father's business? After all, Father God (who created us in His image) Knows Best!

NUMBERS 6:24-26
AARON'S PRIESTLY BLESSING

[24] The Lord bless you and keep you; [25] the Lord make his face shine upon you and be gracious to you; [26] the Lord turn his face toward you and give you peace.

Made in the USA
Columbia, SC
10 December 2022